UNDERSTAND
Revised Edi

This No Nonsense Guide explains

★ How you can plan for a secure retirement

★ The changes in the tax law that affect IRAs

★ How to get the most out of your IRA

THE NO NONSENSE LIBRARY

NO NONSENSE FINANCIAL GUIDES

How to Finance Your Child's College Education, Revised Edition
How to Use Credit and Credit Cards, Revised Edition
Understanding Tax-Exempt Bonds, Revised Edition
Understanding Money Market Funds, Revised Edition
Understanding Mutual Funds, Revised Edition
Understanding IRAs, Revised Edition
Understanding Treasury Bills and Other U.S. Government Securities, Revised Edition
Understanding Common Stocks, Revised Edition
Understanding the Stock Market, Revised Edition
Understanding Stock Options and Futures Markets, Revised Edition
How to Choose a Discount Stockbroker, Revised Edition
How to Make Personal Financial Planning Work for You, Revised Edition
How to Plan and Invest for Your Retirement, Revised Edition
The New Tax Law and What It Means to You

NO NONSENSE REAL ESTATE GUIDES

Understanding Condominiums and Co-ops, Revised Edition
Understanding Buying and Selling a House, Revised Edition
Understanding Mortgages and Home Equity Loans, Revised Edition
Refinancing Your Mortgage, Revised Edition

NO NONSENSE LEGAL GUIDES

Understanding Estate Planning and Wills, Revised Edition
How to Choose a Lawyer

NO NONSENSE CAREER GUIDES

How to Use Your Time Wisely
Managing People

NO NONSENSE SUCCESS GUIDES

NO NONSENSE HEALTH GUIDES

NO NONSENSE COOKING GUIDES

NO NONSENSE WINE GUIDES

NO NONSENSE PARENTING GUIDES

NO NONSENSE FINANCIAL GUIDE®

UNDERSTANDING IRAs

Revised Edition

Arnold Corrigan
& Phyllis C. Kaufman

LONGMEADOW PRESS

Understanding IRAs

Cover designed by Adrian Taylor.
Production services by William S. Konecky Associates, New York

ISBN: 0-681-40251-2

Printed in the United States of America

0 9 8 7 6 5 4 3 2 1

CONTENTS

1 · INTRODUCTION

Would you like to save enough money to enjoy a comfortable retirement?

Would you like to watch your money accumulate, without being taxed each year?

Would you like to see your savings grow ahead of inflation instead of falling behind?

If you are an American taxpayer who works for a living, the best answer to all these questions is likely to be an IRA—an Individual Retirement Account.

If you are wondering whether to start an IRA—or what kind of IRA to start—this book is for you. It's designed to show you the best way to make your IRA grow and help you achieve your personal retirement goals.

And if you have already started an IRA, this book also is for you. It will show you the best ways of *managing* your IRA to make it grow and to take you a long way toward a secure future.

2 · WHAT IS AN IRA?

IRA stands for *Individual Retirement Account*—a type of savings-for-retirement account that provides you with special tax advantages.

A Bit of History

Before 1982, IRAs were only available to people who were not covered by any other type of retirement plan, and the amount of money that could be put in an IRA each year was limited to $1500.

The Economic Recovery and Tax Act of 1981 changed all this. Beginning in 1982, the Act made IRAs available to everyone with earned income (irrespective of any other retirement plan) and raised the yearly contribution limit to $2,000. Taxpayers responded dramatically. By early 1987, the value of all existing IRAs was estimated at *over $300 billion*.

The Double Tax Advantage

The growth of the IRA was based on two great tax advantages:

(1) Under the 1981 law, every working person could put up to $2,000 a year into an IRA and take an immediate tax deduction for the amount contributed. In effect, the taxpayer paid no income tax on the portion of income invested in an IRA.

(2) Even more important, once the money is inside an IRA, it earns and accumulates without being taxed each year. The tax is deferred until the money is withdrawn— which, for savers starting young, may be as much as thirty or forty years in the future. Over the years, this *tax-deferred growth* becomes a far greater advantage, in dollar terms, than the original tax deduction.

The Rules Change Again

The Tax Reform Act of 1986 made new changes to the IRA rules. As we will see in the next chapter, the new law preserved the IRA tax deduction for some taxpayers while eliminating or reducing it for others. But the law left intact the greatest advantage of the IRA—the *tax-deferred growth* that lets you save and invest for the future with no income tax to pay on the earnings until the money is eventually withdrawn.

3 · IRAs AND THE TAX REFORM ACT OF 1986

The Tax Reform Act of 1986 preserved the basic structure of IRAs, including the crucial feature of tax-deferred growth. The law still permits every working person to contribute up to $2,000 annually to an IRA ($2,250 in the case of spousal IRAs—see Chapter 6). And the money in your IRA continues to *earn and compound tax free.*

But beginning with the 1987 tax year, the *tax deduction* for IRA contributions is no longer universal. Instead, the deduction is available to some taxpayers but not to others, depending on (a) the size of your income and (b) whether or not you are covered under any other retirement plan.

The New Deduction Rules

The rules are basically simple:

1. If you are single and *not covered by any employer retirement plan*, then your IRA contribution is *fully tax-deductible*, just as it was before 1987. This is true regardless of your income level.

For married persons filing a joint tax return, the IRA deduction is available without restriction only if *neither spouse* is covered by an employer's retirement plan. If either spouse is covered, then both spouses are subject to income limitations on their IRA deductions, as described below.

The definition of employer retirement plans is broad, including corporate plans, Keogh plans, government plans, tax-sheltered annuities, SEP-IRAs, etc. What it means to be "covered" or "not covered" is discussed later in this chapter and in Appendix B.

2. If an individual *is* covered by an employer's retirement plan—or for married persons filing a joint return, if either spouse is covered—then the IRA deduction depends

on your income. Here's how it works for persons who have other retirement plan coverage:

(a) A single person with adjusted gross income (AGI) of $25,000 or less can still deduct his/her *entire* IRA contribution. If AGI is more than $35,000, then *no* deduction is permitted. If AGI is between $25,000 and $35,000, the deduction is scaled down on a percentage basis—see Appendix A for details. (For example, a single person with AGI of $30,000 and making a $2,000 IRA contribution could deduct 50% of the contribution, or $1,000.)

(b) For married persons filing a joint return, if their AGI is under $40,000, any contributions made to IRAs by either or both spouses are tax-deductible. If AGI is more than $50,000, no deduction is permitted. Between $40,000 and $50,000, the tax deduction for either or both IRAs is scaled down on a percentage basis. (See Appendix A.)

(c) For a married person filing a separate return and covered by an employer's retirement plan, there is no tax deduction if AGI is $10,000 or more. Between 0 and $10,000 of AGI, the tax deduction is scaled down on a percentage basis. If you file a separate return and are not covered by another retirement plan, but your spouse is covered, talk to your accountant or the IRS—the law was subject to change as this book went to press.

What is "AGI"?

For purposes of these IRA calculations, AGI is not quite the same as the "adjusted gross income" most of us recognize from our income tax returns. Instead, it is a "modified adjusted gross income"—the AGI *before* making any deduction for IRA contributions.

Who is "Covered"?

As you can see, it may be critical to know whether you are "covered" under an employer's retirement plan. Usually the distinction is clear; to avoid getting bogged down in legal details, we'll deal with some of the fine points in Appendix B. But it is important to note several situations that do *not* make you "covered." Your IRA deduction is *not* affected simply because you are:

1. Covered under Social Security.
2. Covered under Railroad Retirement.
3. Receiving retirement pension benefit payments.
4. Participating in a government plan as a volunteer fire-fighter.
5. Participating in a government plan as an Armed Forces Reservist who has less than ninety days of active duty during the year.
6. Participating in a "section 457" state or local government deferred compensation plan.

Generally, if you participate in a retirement plan where contributions are made for you on a regular basis, you are covered—or, to use the technical phrase, you are an "active participant." (See Appendix B.)

A Tax Offset

Obviously, many investors will now make contributions to their IRAs that are *not* tax-deductible—contributions of what are termed *after-tax dollars*. Note that if you make nondeductible contributions to an IRA, you will *not* be taxed when you eventually take these same dollars out of your IRA. For the details of how this distribution rule works, see Chapter 7 and Appendix C.

The Bright Side of Tax Reform

There's much more to the Tax Reform Act of 1986 than its effect on the IRA tax deduction. The law eliminates or curtails many previous tax deductions. But it reduces the basic tax rates dramatically, with the top bracket having been cut from 50 percent to 33 percent or 28 percent. For many taxpayers, the lower rates will more than offset the loss of some deductions.

A Specific Improvement

Apart from the change in the tax deduction rules, the Tax Reform Act of 1986 makes relatively few changes in the specific rules governing IRAs. But there's one change that may help people take money *out* of an IRA without a tax penalty. As we will see, the general rule still applies that any money withdrawn from an IRA before age 59½ is subject to a special penalty tax of 10 percent, in addition to regular income tax. But now there's an important exception: distributions can begin before age 59½ without penalty tax, if payment is made in substantially equal installments for the life (or life expectancy) of the planholder or for the joint lives (or joint life expectancies) of the planholder and his/her beneficiary.

4 · ADVANTAGES OF IRAs

The "Miracle of Compound Interest"

Many people, even those who have had IRAs for years, don't fully appreciate the tremendous advantage an IRA provides after money is invested in the account. Have you heard of the "miracle of compound interest"? You may not believe in miracles, but almost everyone is surprised by the extent to which an investment can increase if interest or dividends are reinvested ("compounded") and the entire account is allowed to grow over many years free from current income tax.

In an ordinary investment, the taxes you pay every year on the dividends or interest in effect subtract substantially from your rate of growth. In an IRA, there are no taxes to pay on the account until the money is withdrawn, and your savings can grow at rates that would be almost impossible for you to achieve otherwise.

Over the long run, this *tax-free compounding* will do more for your money than an initial tax deduction. As an illustration, let's assume that an investor makes a $2,000 IRA contribution in a fixed-income investment paying a steady 10 percent return and compounding annually, tax free. A second investor invests the same $2,000 *without* an IRA; assume that he or she is in the 28 percent tax bracket, which means that every year the government takes its share: 28 percent (tax rate) × 10 percent (investment return) = 2.8 percent (tax bite); so that only 7.2 percent of the total 10 percent is left to compound. A third investor is in the 33 percent tax bracket, so that his or her nonsheltered $2,000 compounds at only 6.7 percent. Here is how the same $2,000 would grow in each case:

| | Growth Rate | | |
Value after:	10% (IRA)	7.2% (28% tax bracket)	6.7% (33% tax bracket)
1 Year	$2,200	$2,144	$2,134
5 Years	3,221	2,831	2,766
10 Years	5,187	4,008	3,825
15 Years	8,354	5,675	5,290
20 Years	13,455	8,034	7,317
30 Years	34,899	16,102	13,995
40 Years	90,518	32,272	26,767

You can see the dramatic difference that the extra 2.8 percent or 3.3 percent makes. It's true that the IRA investor still has to pay taxes when the money is finally taken out. (This may be offset, however, by the tax deduction obtained at the beginning, assuming you are eligible for it. This deduction hasn't even been taken into account in the example above.)

Note that this table only shows the growth of a $2,000 investment. Later on we'll look at figures showing the possible growth of an IRA when money is put in and accumulated year after year.

All these figures are intended to emphasize that the point of an IRA contribution is not just to take a tax deduction—it's to get your savings dollars into your own personal tax shelter where they can *compound tax free.*

Tax Deferral

When you retire and begin to take money out of your IRA, you will pay ordinary income tax on the amount withdrawn. So the tax is only deferred, not eliminated. But the table above shows the dramatic growth in your retirement

9

nest egg that this deferral makes possible. And for many people, deferring the tax on this income until after retirement carries an additional benefit, since most of us are likely to be in a lower tax bracket after we retire, and the tax bite consequently will be smaller.

And Perhaps a Deduction

Depending on the factors described in Chapter 3, you may still be eligible to take a current tax deduction for your IRA contribution. If so, the IRA obviously will have even greater advantages for you. The tax deduction will give you extra money to use or invest outside your IRA. If invested, this extra money can add substantially to your total cash buildup.

Freedom of Choice

Finally, consider the IRA's flexibility. There are certain investments, such as tax-exempt bonds, which compound tax free without the need for any special type of account. But with an IRA, you can *choose* your investments from among a great range of possibilities, including many with higher long-term growth rates, and still enjoy the tremendous tax-free compounding advantage. With an IRA, your investment opportunities are almost unlimited. (In Chapter 9, we'll begin to explore where your IRA savings have the best opportunity of growing into a rich retirement.) The power to choose your own investments is a great advantage of the IRA over most other retirement plans. You *control and manage* your own IRA. You can invest your savings for the future effectively, and you can manage your IRA in a way to protect you against inflation in the years ahead.

5 · DISADVANTAGES OF IRAs

Since there are two sides to every question, there must be disadvantages to IRAs as well as advantages. True?

As an old professor of philosophy once taught us, there are not necessarily two sides to every question. And there are surprisingly few disadvantages to IRAs. But, yes, there are some.

First, as we saw in Chapter 3, many individuals can no longer enjoy a current income tax deduction for their IRA contributions. We've pointed out that the tax-free compounding of your money in an IRA may be more important than the original tax deduction. But it's obviously even better if you can get a tax deduction too. As we will see in Chapter 17, there may be alternatives where some people can get both advantages.

Another concern of many people is the fear of "locking up" their money in a retirement plan, and then not being able to get their money out if they need it. In Chapter 8, we will see that with an IRA, this problem is quite manageable. There's a penalty for taking money out before age 59½, but the penalty is not prohibitive. Moreover, as a result of the Tax Reform Act of 1986, there's a way to begin taking IRA distributions before age 59½ without paying the penalty tax.

So the fear of being "locked in" usually should not stop you from having an IRA. Of course there are exceptions: If the only money that you can come up with for an IRA is money you know you will need to spend in a year or two, there's no sense putting it in an IRA.

There's a related point that isn't really a disadvantage, but that does stop many people from beginning an IRA. Many young people feel that retirement is so distant that they simply can't see the need to start a retirement plan right away. Who knows what the world will be like thirty or forty years from now, and why try to plan for it? It's easy to feel that way. But as this book will show you, an IRA is not only a retirement plan, but also a *savings* plan that can do a surprising amount for your financial future even if you take out part or all of the money long before retirement. As we said, it's a tax shelter for everyone. That's hard to beat.

A much more specific IRA disadvantage is the way the money is taxed when you do take it out. As we will see, all normal distributions from IRAs are taxed as "ordinary income." That may seem reasonable enough, but in certain non-IRA retirement plans, by contrast, you are eligible for a special tax break if you take the money out in a lump sum. In Chapter 17 we will discuss what you should do if one of these alternatives is available where you work. But if your choice is between an IRA and an ordinary non-IRA savings program—then the IRA wins on almost all counts, and the taxes you pay at the end shouldn't be regarded as a disadvantage.

In Chapter 18, we will talk about the specific "do's" and "dont's" that apply to IRAs. If you are comparing an IRA to an alternative retirement plan, some of these prohibitions may matter. For example, you can borrow from certain retirement plans, but not from an IRA. Certain other plans let you make larger contributions, and you may have more flexibility in postponing the time when you must begin to withdraw money. If any of these choices is important to you, you should certainly consider other available plans carefully.

But for most of us, the choice is between using an IRA as a personal tax shelter, and having no tax shelter at all. When you compare the advantages of an IRA with the disadvantages, the advantages are overwhelming.

6 · PUTTING MONEY IN

This chapter will review the legal limitations on how much and when you can put money in your IRA. The basic rules governing contributions and withdrawals from an IRA were established by Congress in the Economic Recovery and Tax Act of 1981. The various institutions that "sponsor" or offer IRA plans to the public also have their own rules on certain points, particularly on the minimum amounts that can be contributed—you should of course check the rules of a particular plan before you begin. (Which of the many available types of IRAs to choose will be discussed in Chapters 9–14.)

Who is Eligible?

An IRA is for everyone who has "earned income"—everyone who works for a living.

As we pointed out in Chapter 2, before 1982 the IRA was only for persons who were not covered by any other retirement plan. But beginning in 1982, IRAs became available to everyone with earned income. Now you can have an IRA in addition to any other retirement plans under which you are covered (corporate, government, or self-employed). Participation in another retirement plan may affect your tax deduction, but it does not stop you from having an IRA.

But note that an IRA can be based only on *earned* income—income you earn by your personal efforts—wages, salaries, commissions, bonuses, tips, self-employment, etc. And note that *alimony* counts as earned income for IRA purposes. But income from interest, dividends, rents or royalties doesn't count as earned income. Neither does pension income of any sort, or gifts.

How Much Can I Put In?

For an individual, the maximum that you can put in your IRA ("contribute") is $2,000 annually. But you can't contribute more than your earned income. If your earned income is only $1,500, your contribution limit is $1,500. Looking at it the other way, if you earn $2,000 or less you can contribute your entire yearly earnings to your IRA.

What is the Minimum Contribution?

The law doesn't set any minimum. The various IRA sponsors, such as banks and mutual funds, generally do set minimums, but the minimums are usually quite low and well within reach.

Must My Contributions Be Regular?

As long as you stay within the maximum limit ($2,000), you have complete flexibility with regard to your IRA contributions. You can contribute as little as you like for a given year, or not at all. You can contribute $2,000 one year, $500 the next, and nothing at all the third. But whenever you contribute less than the permitted limit in one year, you can't make up the lost amount in a following year. That particular opportunity to put the $2,000 maximum into your IRA tax shelter is lost forever.

How Do IRAs Work for Husband and Wife?

If both spouses have earned income, each can have a separate IRA, and each can put in up to $2,000 (but not more than his or her earned income). It doesn't matter whether they file a joint federal income tax return or separate returns.

If one spouse has little or no earned income, the higher-earning spouse can have a regular IRA and a separate "spousal IRA" can be set up for the low-earning (or nonworking) spouse. Total yearly contributions of up to

$2,250 can be made to the two accounts. This total can be split in any way desired, except that neither account can receive more than $2,000 in any year. The two IRAs function independently in most other respects and are managed like any other IRAs, but the couple must file a joint tax return.

What are the Age Limits?

The upper limit for IRA contributions is age 70½. Specifically, you cannot make an IRA contribution in the calendar year in which you reach age 70½. (And the following year is the year in which withdrawals from an IRA must begin. See Chapter 7.)

There's no lower age limit for an IRA. A teenager or even a young child with earnings can have an IRA. The possible tax deduction may not seem important then, but having the money in a tax shelter can have dramatic results over the years.

In a spousal IRA, the upper age limit applies separately to each spouse. No contribution may be made to the spousal IRA of a low-earning or nonworking spouse who has reached age 70½, but the working spouse is still entitled to a contribution of up to $2,000 if he or she is under the age limit. If the working spouse is over the age limit but the nonworking spouse is not, a contribution of up to $2,000 may be made to the IRA of the nonworking spouse only.

When Can Contributions Be Made?

You can open an IRA or contribute to an existing IRA at any time during the year or until April 15 of the following year. Even if you have obtained an extension beyond April 15 for filing your tax return, your IRA contribution must still be made by April 15. You can file your return early and claim an IRA deduction (if you are eligible for a deduction) even if the contribution hasn't yet been made, as long as the contribution is then made by April 15.

You can contribute in a lump sum or in installments, to the extent permitted by the type of investment you have chosen. But remember that your IRA money compounds tax free. *The earlier in the year you make your contribution, the sooner your money begins to benefit from the tax-free compounding.*

What About Taking the Tax Deduction?

If you are eligible (see Chapter 3), you can take the federal tax deduction for your IRA contribution whether or not you itemize other deductions on your tax return. There are special lines on page 1 of Form 1040 (the long form) for entering deductible IRA contributions. On the 1987 tax forms, you can also take the IRA deduction on Form 1040A (the short form), but not on Form 1040EZ (the extra-simple form).

What About State Income Taxes?

The rules for taking deductions on state income taxes vary from state to state. The majority of states allow the same deduction as on your federal return. Some don't. Check the tax forms and rules in your own state.

What If I Overcontribute?

If you find that through some error you have contributed more than $2,000 in a given year, or more than your earned income, there are two relatively easy solutions. The first alternative is to withdraw the excess amount, along with any additional amount that has been earned on this excess, before the April 15 deadline. If there are any earnings, you are taxed on these at regular rates, plus a 10 percent penalty tax if you are under age 59½. The second alternative is to leave the excess in and let it be credited as a contribution for the next year; in this case you pay a modest penalty of 6 percent of the amount of the excess for each year that it remains as excess. (Normally this would be only for one year, and the 6 percent would hardly be enough to worry about.)

What If I Can't Afford to Contribute?

Obviously, you want to put as much money in your IRA as you can afford each year—not only if you are eligible for the tax deduction, but because any part of the $2,000 limit that you don't use does not carry over to following years. But what if you haven't been able to put aside the cash? There are two possible solutions:

The good solution is to look over all your existing investments carefully. Do you have a long-term savings account? Or stocks or bonds that you are holding for long-term investment? Consider taking $2,000 out of one of these nest eggs and putting it in your IRA (assuming that you have had enough earned income during the year to justify the IRA contribution). You may be eligible to get the IRA tax deduction; the money is still working for you long-term; and better still, it is working for you in a tax shelter where it can compound tax free until withdrawn. However, consider that if you sell an existing investment, you may have to pay a capital gains tax on the sale.

The statistics indicate that millions of investors have taken this way of financing their IRA contributions. While it may not fulfill the government's goal of encouraging additional saving, there is no reason why it can't work just fine for you.

The other solution to contributing to an IRA when you don't have ready cash is not as desirable, but it's worth mentioning. There's no rule against *borrowing* to put money in an IRA. If you are without cash this year but expect to have enough extra in the next year or two, you can borrow now, make your IRA contribution, take the tax deduction if you are eligible, and pay the money back to the lender later on. Some banks are encouraging this kind of loan. But note that if you are short of cash and have to withdraw money from your IRA to repay the loan, there will be certain restrictions if you are under age 59½ (see Chapter 8). Note also that you may not *pledge* any part of your IRA as collateral for a loan.

7 · TAKING MONEY OUT

Let's hope that you will not need to withdraw money from your IRA for a long time—that you will be able to make sizable contributions each year and let them accumulate until retirement. But sooner or later, you will begin withdrawing money from your IRA. Here are the rules for taking money out:

When Can I Take Money Out?

There are two key ages for planning IRA withdrawals—age 59½ and age 70½.

If you take any money out of your IRA before the day that you reach age 59½, you pay a flat penalty tax of 10 percent of the amount withdrawn (in addition to ordinary income tax on the amount). The penalty tax generally applies unless you die or become disabled before age 59½. However, there's another exception which we'll discuss later in this chapter and in Chapter 8.

What Happens After Age 59½?

You aren't forced to take withdrawals from your IRA until age 70½. Between ages 59½ and 70½, you have great flexibility. You can withdraw money from your IRA without restrictions; or, if you are still working, you can keep making contributions (prior to the year in which you reach age 70½). As your needs change from time to time, you can do both. For information on how withdrawals are taxed, see below.

Does It Matter When I Actually Retire?

Although IRA is short for Individual Retirement Account, there isn't really much of a tie-in with actual retirement. The law only talks about the specified age limits. After age

59½, you can withdraw money without penalty from your IRA even if you are still working. Of course, if you are retired and have no earned income, you can't make further IRA contributions.

What Happens at Age 70½?

The IRS doesn't want you to postpone withdrawals indefinitely. Beginning by April 1 of the year following the year in which you reach age 70½, you *must* withdraw at least a certain amount annually based on your life expectancy, or the joint life expectancy of you and your spouse (or other beneficiary). For example, if you are a single person aged 71, the IRS figures your life expectancy to be 15.3 years (based on the 1987 tables). If your spouse is the same age, your joint life expectancy is placed at 19.8 years. If you have $400,000 in your IRA at that age, the minimum annual withdrawal for the first year would be calculated as follows:

Alone	With Spouse
$400,000	$400,000
÷15.3	÷19.8
=$26,144	=$20,202

Life expectancy tables can be found in IRS publications 590 (IRAs) and 575 (Pension and Annuity Income), available in most libraries and through your local IRS office. But don't be too concerned over the calculation of your required withdrawals. Most IRAs operate with a bank as trustee or custodian, and the bank will usually help you set a withdrawal schedule when you reach age 70½. Or this function may be performed by the IRA plan sponsor.

The required distribution for each year generally must be made by December 31 of that year; the first year deadline (the following April 1) is an exception. Take as an example a person who reaches age 70½ in 1990 and plans to take the minimum required distributions. For this person, the deadlines for completing each year's distribution will be as follows:

1st year	April 1, 1991
2nd year	December 31, 1991
3rd year	December 31, 1992
4th year	December 31, 1993
	and so on.

Many people take money out of their IRAs before age 70½, and many take more than the required minimums. But the required minimum calculation is important to anyone who wants to minimize taxes by taking the least possible amount out of his/her IRA, and leaving the maximum amount in the IRA to earn and compound tax free.

How Are Distributions Taxed?

The tax rules concerning distributions are very simple: with one important exception (see below), withdrawals from an IRA (called "IRA distributions") are taxed as ordinary income. If you take the money out in installments, you pay tax each year only on the amount actually withdrawn. A lump-sum distribution from an IRA does *not* qualify for special tax treatment (unlike lump-sum distributions from corporate or other "qualified" retirement plans, which may be taxed under a special formula that can reduce the tax). So once you have met any minimum distribution requirement, there is usually no reason to take more out of your IRA in any given year than you actually need, unless your tax rate in that year will be lower than in following years.

The important exception is as follows: if you have made *nondeductible* contributions to your IRA, then a part of your total withdrawals, equal to the total dollar amount of those nondeductible contributions, will be withdrawn without tax. Any *earnings* on the nondeductible contributions, however, are taxed on withdrawal. The IRS provides a worksheet for calculating what part of any IRA distribution is nontaxable. Basically, the nontaxable portion depends on the ratio of your past nondeductible contributions to the current market value of your IRA(s). For more details on this calculation, see Appendix C.

An important note: If you make withdrawals before age 59½, any nontaxable portion of your distributions is exempt from the 10 percent penalty tax, just as it is exempt from ordinary income tax.

Tax Withholding on Distributions

There's a rule under which a certain percentage of any IRA distribution is supposed to be withheld for Federal income tax. But if you don't want this withholding to apply, it's easy to request an exemption by filing a simple form. The sponsor or custodian of your IRA is required to give you enough warning time to apply for this exemption if you wish.

Of course, avoiding the withholding doesn't mean that you avoid the tax. The less tax you have withheld during the year, the more you may owe at the end. And you may also run afoul of the estimated tax rules, which require in most cases that a substantial part of your tax be paid during the year, rather than waiting until the end.

What If I Die?

If you die before you begin to take withdrawals from your IRA, or before the withdrawals are completed, the balance in your account passes to your beneficiary. To avoid complications, we strongly recommend that you file a "designation of beneficiary" form with the trustee or custodian of your IRA. If you have any doubts or questions about your choice of beneficiary, we suggest talking to an attorney. And when an IRA planholder dies, the beneficiary or beneficiaries may gain by talking to an attorney or accountant about possible choices of distribution options. Payments to a beneficiary, like any other distribution from an IRA, are taxed as ordinary income when received (except for any adjustment for past nondeductible contributions).

What If I Become Permanently Disabled?

If you become disabled—and you should check with the IRS to see if you meet their definition of this term—you can take money out of your IRA before age 59½ without paying a penalty tax. But you still pay ordinary income tax on the amount withdrawn.

The Extra Reward

Assuming that you stay alive to enjoy your IRA, there is an extra reward waiting for you that you may not have thought about.

You may have seen tables projecting how much you can accumulate in an IRA by age 59½, or 65, or 70½. But let's assume that at whatever age you start to withdraw, you can afford to withdraw gradually—perhaps at the minimum required rates that we discussed earlier in this chapter.

The extra reward is that while you are taking the money out in installments, the balance left in your IRA continues to earn and compound tax free. If your money is invested in an IRA that is earning a high rate of return (see Chapter 9), it's quite possible that your money may earn as much in the first few years of withdrawals as you are taking out. And in that case, it's also possible that the amounts you take out could get larger every year.

8 · DEALING WITH THE PENALTY TAX

Many people, especially young people, are afraid of "locking up" money until retirement. And the penalty tax on withdrawals under age 59½ adds to these fears.

Usually, you shouldn't let this worry stand in your way. The IRA is remarkably flexible. If you do have to take out money before age 59½, your IRA isn't disqualified in any way, and no special restrictions are placed on the money that remains in the account. You simply pay the 10 percent penalty tax on the amount withdrawn (in addition to paying ordinary income tax). And, as we'll see below, there's now a way to take some money out before age 59½ without paying a penalty at all.

What if you do pay the penalty tax? All in all, the 10 percent penalty rate is quite moderate. First, let's assume that you have gotten the benefit of a tax deduction on your IRA contributions. In this case, once the money has been in your IRA for five or six years, you have probably gained enough by the tax-free compounding to make up for the penalty tax on any part of the money that you choose to take out. If the money has been in your IRA for seven years or more, you almost certainly come out ahead despite the tax. (Obviously, if you are well under age 59½, it doesn't make sense to put money in an IRA that you know you will need within two or three years.)

If your contributions have been *nondeductible*, the penalty tax can never put you very far behind, since, as we saw in Chapter 7, the penalty tax isn't applied to these contributions when withdrawn, but only to the *earnings* on these contributions.

Pre-59½ Withdrawals Without Penalty

Prior to the Tax Reform Act of 1986, the 10 percent penalty tax applied to all IRA withdrawals before age 59½ except in case of death or disability. But the 1986 Act made an important exception that lets you get at part of your IRA before age 59½ without penalty.

Under the new rule, you can avoid the premature withdrawal penalty by taking a series of *substantially equal periodic payments* based on your life expectancy, or the joint life expectancies of you and your beneficiary.

The payments must occur at least once a year and must continue for at least five years or until you turn age 59½, whichever is later. If the payment plan is modified before the end of the later of these periods, the IRS will retroactively assess the 10 percent penalty on all amounts received. But after the end of the five-year period, or when you reach age 59½, whichever is later, you can discontinue the payments or vary the plan.

One of the situations where the new rule may be helpful is if you are under age 59½ and are considering rolling over a distribution from a qualified plan into an IRA. (See Chapter 16 on rollovers.) Previously, you might have considered only a partial rollover in order to keep a portion of the money outside the IRA for other expenses. Now, you may find it workable to roll over the entire amount and to take small distributions directly from the IRA under the new rule.

How the Withdrawals Are Calculated

The basic method for determining the permitted size of your pre-59½ payments is to divide the amount in your IRA by your life expectancy, which may be recalculated each year. For example, at age 50, with a $100,000 IRA and an actuarial life expectancy of 33.1 years (according to the 1987 IRS tables), your first distribution will be $3,021 ($100,000 divided by 33.1).

For the next year, your life expectancy will be a lower number and the amount in your IRA will probably change due to investment results. The withdrawal from your IRA can be recalculated each year based on these factors.

If your IRA is growing at a good rate, the payments are likely to get larger from year to year. Still, as you can see from the above figures, the initial distributions will be small relative to the size of your IRA. Accordingly, it is possible that the IRS may provide more liberal alternate payout schedules. If you are thinking of taking advantage of this provision of the law, check with your accountant and/or the IRS.

9 · WHERE TO INVEST YOUR IRA MONEY— AN OVERVIEW

By now, if you don't already have an IRA, we hope you are impressed with the advantages of having one. An IRA is flexible. It gives you a tax shelter for the future to help your money grow. It may give you a tax deduction. It stays with you when you move from one job to another, and it is under your control.

But we have hardly touched on the most important aspect of an IRA: First and foremost, an IRA is an *investment*. For many people, it will be the most important investment they ever make.

In the future, many people will retire relying on some combination of (1) Social Security, (2) a private pension plan, and (3) their own IRA. Of these three, the IRA is the only one that is totally under your control. In an IRA, you have the power to make the decisions. It is no exaggeration to say that the way you use this power can make a major difference in your financial future.

We want to stress that if you have looked at an IRA only as a tax deduction, you are missing the main attraction. The same holds true if you have lost the deduction under tax reform and think that you shouldn't contribute to an IRA anymore. An IRA is, or should be, an *investment plan*. By letting your investment earn, compound and grow *tax free* until retirement, the government gives this kind of investment plan an advantage that can be enormous over the years.

Growth Investments and Income Investments

Traditionally, investments are usually categorized as being either for "growth" of your money or for "current spendable income." Obviously, current income isn't an objective in the years when you are building up your IRA. However, certain so-called income investments may turn out to be your choice. This is because the difference between growth and income investments is largely one of *risk*.

In *growth* investments, you take more risks and accept more uncertainties in the hope of eventually making more money. In growth investments you are usually an *owner*. The value of your investment may fluctuate according to the stock market, industry trends or world affairs. Because prices fluctuate, you won't want to run the extra risk of being forced to sell a good growth investment when prices happen to be low. So these investments should be for the long run—for money that you won't need currently.

Income investments are generally intended to avoid dramatic gains or losses and to give you a steady, reliable flow of income. Often you are a *lender* rather than an owner. But note that you don't have to *spend* the income. If you plow it back in and let it accumulate (and earn *more* income), you now have an investment that will *grow*—not dramatically, but at a rate that hopefully will be reasonably predictable and subject only to gradual changes.

Now, you must analyze your needs and what we might call your investment personality. Will you be content only with safe, secure, stable investments? If so, you should aim to put your IRA money in the so-called income investments. Or, are you willing to try for greater rewards, and risk some uncertainty and price fluctuations and even possible losses? If putting all your money in growth investments seems too risky, how about a combination of both?

In the next chapters we will describe the various IRA investment opportunities. Which one, or ones, you choose depends on your investment approach. In choosing between more risk and less risk, there's no clear right or wrong answer—the answer has to be one that suits you, and one that you can live with.

Risk and Reward

But why should anyone take risks with hard-earned money? The answer to that question, which many people ask, can probably be given more easily in numbers than in words.

More About Tax-Free Compounding

We have talked about the advantages of tax-free compounding, and in Chapter 4 we gave figures to show how it helps your money grow. That table also made another point. It showed that a higher earnings rate—say 10 percent instead of 7 percent—makes a truly phenomenal difference in your results over longer time periods.

Different kinds of investments earn at different rates. So the choice of your IRA investment is worth time and serious thought on your part.

To illustrate the point further, here are a few more figures on how an investment grows at different earnings rates. Let's say, for simplicity, that several investors invest $1,000 each at rates varying from 5 percent to 14 percent. Note that the difference after one year is slight—after five years it's still moderate—but as the years go on, even a small difference in rates makes a very big difference in how the $1,000 grows:

| Number of Years | Growth Rate | | | | | |
	5%	6%	8%	10%	12%	14%
1 Year	$1,050	$1,060	$1,080	$1,100	$1,120	$1,140
5 Years	1,276	1,338	1,469	1,611	1,762	1,925
10 Years	1,629	1,791	2,159	2,594	3,106	3,707
20 Years	2,653	3,207	4,661	6,727	9,646	13,743
30 Years	4,322	5,743	10,063	17,449	29,960	50,950
40 Years	7,040	10,286	21,725	45,259	93,051	188,884

So there may be good reason to take some risks in the hope of achieving a higher return. But you may just as legitimately be concerned with safety. You may be willing to give up some growth potential in order to know that your investment will increase at a reasonably steady rate and will not show sharp fluctuations in value. You might easily take this point of view if you are only a few years away from retirement and want to be sure of how many dollars you will have in your fund when you are ready to begin withdrawals. Or you may see a possible need for an emergency withdrawal from your IRA, and one of your objectives may be to keep part or all of your IRA fairly liquid—i.e., easily convertible into cash.

You will find, or very likely you have already found, that there are countless institutions out there willing and able to take your IRA dollars. But where should you put those dollars? The choices range from no risk at all to very high risk indeed. Keeping in mind just how critical your investment choices will be, in the following chapters we will look carefully at the alternatives.

10 · BANK IRAs

Banks were the most aggressive promoters of IRAs after the law changed in 1982, and they have led the parade in terms of numbers of IRAs opened and dollars invested. For convenience, we will use the term "banks" to cover a whole group of institutions that operate in a similar fashion as far as your IRA investment is concerned—commercial banks, savings banks, savings and loan associations, and credit unions.

A Bit of History

What do you get in a bank IRA? The packages offered by most banks are probably reasonable for many investors. It wasn't always so. Up until the late 1970s, the interest rates banks paid to their individual depositors were strictly regulated and were often far below what is often called the "market rate" of interest. The market rate is the interest rate that governments, banks and major corporations pay when they borrow money for short periods. But since 1978, the limits on the rates banks can pay their depositors have largely been abolished. Thanks to deregulation and competition, individual savers are now paid at rates that are roughly in line with these market rates.

This assumes, of course, that you avoid the old-style bank "passbook" savings accounts that still only pay around 5½ percent. For some reason, there are still billions of dollars in these accounts, including many that could easily meet the minimum requirements for one of the newer, higher-paying accounts. Old habits die hard.

If you put your IRA dollars in a bank and take advantage of the best interest rates that the bank offers, what will this do for you over the long run?

The answer is surprisingly simple. No one can be completely certain of the future. But, based on past experience, if your money earns interest at rates roughly in line with the market rates, then, over the long run, *your money will probably grow enough to keep up with inflation and perhaps a little more.*

Inflation and Interest

Let us explain. Each year, the real value of your dollars—that is, their purchasing power—shrinks because of inflation. But experience shows that generally, if you earn market interest rates, you will add enough dollars over the years to make up for the shrinkage. The adjustment is rough, and there may be times when interest rates and inflation seem to be completely out of line with each other, but the long-run relationship makes sense, if you think about it. For example, if the inflation rate is 5 percent, the institutions that lend money on a large scale will be reluctant to lend unless they get a minimum interest rate of 5 percent—enough to offset the shrinkage in the real value of their money due to inflation.

On the average, more often than not, market interest rates will be a little *above* the rate of inflation. This premium is what economists refer to as the "real rate" of interest—the interest rate that money earns after you take out the inflation factor.

In the 1970s and 1980s, inflation and interest rates have at times soared to unprecedented levels, and there have been times when the real rate of interest—the margin of the interest rate over the inflation rate—was much higher than in the past. No one knows yet whether this marks a change in the long-run pattern, or whether it is only a temporary development. You should watch the trend; but for the present, it is probably wise to assume that money in the bank will still earn only a small premium above the rate of inflation.

This shouldn't be disappointing or discouraging. In the 1970s, when inflation was rising but bank interest rates were still tightly controlled and unfavorable to the small investor, money in the bank lost much of its real value even when all the interest was plowed back in. That's much less likely to happen in the future, assuming that you take advantage of the higher earning accounts. Each dollar you put in the bank will almost certainly lose value from year to year due to inflation, but your greater interest earnings should add enough to the number of dollars to make up for the shrinkage—and probably a little bit more.

Why a Bank IRA?

What are the advantages of a bank IRA? Your money is *safe*—you know the dollars you have put there, plus whatever interest is earned, are locked away safely. Bank managements vary in quality, but you can sleep soundly, because your account is insured up to $100,000 by the FDIC (Federal Deposit Insurance Corporation) or, in the case of a savings and loan, by the FSLIC (Federal Savings and Loan Insurance Corporation).

Also, banks are convenient and familiar. Their minimum dollar requirements for starting an IRA are usually very low (but be careful, because very small accounts may earn only the lower "passbook" interest rate). And the banks usually charge a very low fee for handling your IRA, or often no fee at all.

Who should have a bank IRA? We will talk below about other investments that can make your money grow more than is possible in a bank account. But some people are not comfortable with the uncertainties and risks of a growth investment. If you simply can't sleep well without a government guarantee of your money, then by all means be content with a bank IRA.

Others may have specific reasons for wanting the complete safety of a bank. If you are very near retirement and want to be sure that all your dollars will be there when you are ready to withdraw, a bank IRA gives you that certainty. The same is true if you are younger but see the possibility that you may have to make emergency withdrawals.

Which Bank and Which Type of Account

If you do want the security of a bank IRA, which particular bank and which type of account? You will have to do some comparison shopping. Pick a bank whose rates look good and which gives you a reasonable choice of types of certificates and accounts.

There are two primary types of bank investments for your IRA: money market deposit accounts, which run without time limit, and certificates of deposit, for specific time periods.

Money market deposit accounts (also called market rate accounts) came into existence in 1982 to let the banks compete more effectively with the money market funds. The minimum deposit needed to earn the full rate on these accounts in many banks is $2,500 or more, but for an IRA, the minimum may be as little as $500. Since there is no maturity date, these accounts are fully liquid—you can take out your money at any time without any bank penalty for early withdrawal.

A money market deposit account is a convenient choice for any IRA money that you expect to be withdrawing in the very near future. Or, if you are considering switching all or part of your money to a different type of IRA, a money market deposit account makes an excellent temporary resting place (see Chapter 15). The rates paid on these accounts are set arbitrarily by each bank and vary from bank to bank, but they are usually reasonably close to those paid by the banks' archrivals, the money market funds.

The various *certificates of deposit,* or "CDs," offered by the banks for periods of six months, one year or longer will generally give you higher rates than the money market deposit accounts, but there's a penalty if you take your money out before the maturity date. On a certificate of one year or longer, the minimum penalty is loss of three months' interest. On shorter-term certificates the penalty may be smaller. However, some banks don't impose these penalties on an IRA holder who has reached age 59½.

If you intend to leave your IRA money in the bank anyway, the penalty feature of these certificates shouldn't be a practical problem. However, note that buying a longer-term certificate involves a modest interest rate risk. If interest rates rise after you buy a long-term certificate, you will be sorry that you didn't wait longer to invest. On the other hand, if interest rates drop, you will be glad that you are assured of the higher rate for a specific period.

If you buy a longer-term certificate, and interest rates then do rise sharply, it may be worth paying the bank penalty to cash in the old certificate and reinvest in a new certificate carrying a higher rate. Let a bank employee help you calculate the difference.

In comparing certificates and other accounts, remember that interest rates work out differently depending on how often the interest is compounded. For each type of account, or certificate, ask the bank for the "effective annual yield." The effective annual yield tells you how much would actually be added to your investment per year by a particular interest arrangement, whether the compounding is daily (the most favorable), quarterly, semiannually or annually. This gives you a fair basis for comparison.

The Interest Rate Dilemma

Once you have made the effective yield comparison, the next step is simple in theory but not so simple in practice. If you think that interest rates are going to drop, you should theoretically buy a long-term certificate to "lock in" the current higher rate. If you think that rates are going up, you should stick to a money market deposit account or a shorter-term certificate so that you will be free to switch when rates do rise.

The trouble is that even the most reputable economists find it terribly difficult to predict movements in interest rates. So if you want to stay out of the very tricky interest rate forecasting business, it is perfectly reasonable to pick whatever certificate gives you the highest effective annual yield now, make a careful note of when it matures, and then not worry about it. If interest rates rise—well, that will benefit you when it's time for next year's IRA contribution.

The Banks Diversify

In this chapter we have talked about the traditional bank offerings to savers, particularly CDs and money market deposit accounts. It's important to note that in recent years, many banks (and particularly certain large banks) have moved beyond their traditional roles and have begun offering mutual funds and/or brokerage accounts to their customers. The mutual funds offered may be existing funds with established track records, or else new funds created particularly for the bank. The brokerage services are usually offered by bank affiliates and are of the no-frills discount brokerage variety. In both cases, the banks have promoted the advantages of these new services to long-term IRA investors.

You may like the convenience of doing business with a bank. But in judging these services, compare the bank mutual funds to independent mutual funds of similar types (see Chapter 13), and compare the brokerage services or "self-directed accounts" to the services available from established discount brokerage firms. In your IRA, you will eventually have a sizable amount of money at stake; so do your comparison shopping carefully.

11 · MONEY MARKET FUND IRAs

From the point of view of your IRA, a money market fund will give you results very similar to those you can obtain from a bank.

A Money Market Fund Is a Type of Mutual Fund

You are probably familiar with money market funds. A money market fund is a type of mutual fund. A "mutual fund" is an organization in which money from thousands of investors, large and small, is pooled so that the money can be handled effectively as a single unit and enjoy such key advantages as professional management and diversification of investments. In a "money market fund," the assets of this pool are invested for maximum safety and liquidity by making low risk, short-term loans to the government and to major banks and corporations at market rates of interest. (For more details see the No Nonsense Financial Guide, *Understanding Money Market Funds.*)

So a money market fund, by its nature, earns the market rate of interest we talked about in Chapter 10, and pays this money out to its shareholders as income after deducting a small amount for the expenses of running the fund. (These payments to shareholders technically are called "dividends," but they simply pass through to the shareholders the *interest* earned by the fund.)

The phenomenal growth of the money market funds began in the late 1970s, when banks were under legal limitations and were still generally paying only 5¼ percent to 5½ percent on savings accounts, while the money market funds were able to offer rates of 10 percent and higher. As the banks gradually deregulated and began to offer higher-paying certificates, the competitive differences between the banks and the money funds narrowed. In December 1982, when the banks were permitted to offer the money market deposit accounts mentioned in Chapter 10, the differences narrowed further.

What will a money market fund do for your IRA? Your earnings will be tied to the market rate of interest even more closely than with a bank, and over the long run *your money will probably grow enough to keep up with inflation and perhaps a little more.* (Yes, we know—that's exactly what we said above about *bank* IRAs.)

Money Market Funds vs. Banks

Obviously, a money market fund IRA will suit exactly the same people who want the advantages offered by banks. You know that the dollars you have put in the account are safe. The interest you earn varies daily, but you know that it will generally reflect the market rate. As with a bank, the safety offered by a money market fund may be particularly attractive if you are near retirement, or anticipate needing cash in an emergency, and want to be sure of the number of dollars you have available.

Comparing a money market fund to a bank money market account for an IRA, there are more similarities than differences. The money market funds have starting minimums of about $1,000 or sometimes as low as $500. The fund's income is calculated daily, and all shareholders receive the same rate, whatever it may be. Also, the money funds generally offer attractive check-writing privileges, but that isn't relevant as far as your IRA is concerned, because your money stays invested and all dividends are plowed back in.

Safety Without Insurance

Unlike bank accounts, the money funds carry no government insurance guarantee. But the safety record of the money funds is perfectly good because their investments are safe, and we don't think that this difference is really significant. If you want the highest degree of safety, you can invest in a money market fund that specializes in U.S. government securities. (You will earn a slightly lower yield than in a regular money market fund.)

Rate of Return

Generally, in recent years, the *average* money market fund has given its shareholders a somewhat higher yield than the *average* bank market rate account. (The return on bank market rate accounts is set arbitrarily by the banks every week, and the banks may have found it unprofitable to match the money market funds completely.) But these are *averages*. You need to do comparison shopping in the large banking centers such as New York City, where bank competition is fierce, and some banks may be paying more than the money market funds.

In a money market fund, your money is never locked in for a specific time period. It is always easily available. That's why it is natural to compare a money market fund with a bank market rate account. But in a money fund, unlike a bank, you can't obtain higher yields by locking up your money in certificates for six months, two years, etc. If you intend to stay with the safest types of investment, these certificates will probably earn more for you over the long run than a market rate account or a money market fund.

On the other hand, the money market fund can offer you the possibility of switching much more extensively among different types of investments. If you pick a money market fund that is part of a larger mutual fund group, you can enjoy the convenience and ease of switching your dollars, say, from a money market fund to a common stock fund and back again. If you want to diversify your IRA among various investments, particularly as your IRA grows larger, this can be a major convenience.

If you want a money market fund but don't care about the switching privilege, the differences among most of the leading funds are not large. The current yields of many of these funds are carried weekly by major newspapers. You want a fund that gives you a reasonably good yield (not necessarily the highest) compared with the group, and one that will give you convenient, efficient services. (See the No Nonsense Financial Guide, *Understanding Money Market Funds.*)

12 · BROKERAGE FIRM IRAs

Having discussed the most conservative means of investing your IRA money, let's jump to the opposite end of the spectrum and look at brokerage firm IRAs.

The terms "broker," "brokerage firm," "stockbroker," "securities broker," "broker-dealer," are all terms that are used to describe the people and firms that sell securities to the public. (For more about brokers and the stock market, see the No Nonsense Financial Guide, *Understanding the Stock Market.*)

If your IRA is invested with a brokerage firm, you have a tremendous range of investments available. Some have the potential of making your money grow far more over the years than is possible with a bank or money market fund IRA. But there is always a trade-off: Investments with higher growth potential also carry more risk and uncertainty. As we said in Chapter 9, in most of these investments you are an *owner* rather than a *lender*, and the value of your investment is likely to fluctuate. You will never be certain of just what the earnings will be in any given year. If the investment is badly chosen, you may suffer a loss.

On the other hand, if the investment is well chosen over the long run, the growth (rewards) may well be worth the risks. Take common stocks, for example. We have said that banks and money market funds will probably earn enough over the long run to keep you even with the rate of inflation, or a little ahead. Over a period of many years, common stock investments, on the average, have grown at an average rate of *6 percent better than the rate of inflation*. By choosing and timing their investments well, several professional investment managers have made common stock accounts grow at rates *8 percent above* the rate of inflation, or even higher. Look at the table on page 28 and think what an additional 6 percent or 8 percent can mean over the life of your IRA.

The Rewards of Patience

So a successful growth investment can reward you handsomely *if you are patient.* But the year-to-year fluctuations can be sharp. Obviously, you need to stay with this type of investment long enough so that the long-run growth trend will outweigh the short-run ups and downs. If you are investing money that you will need in a year or two, you are much better off in a bank or money market fund, where you are free from worry about what your investment will be worth at the time you take it out.

On the other hand, if you expect to maintain your IRA for more than five years—and even more particularly if your time span is more than ten years—then the advantages of a growth investment can be well worth the uncertainties and risks, and you owe it to yourself (and to your future) to consider these investments seriously.

Minimizing Risks

What are the risks? Even the best growth investment is likely to fluctuate in value and earnings from year to year. Apart from these uncertainties, which can be caused by many things such as market and industry conditions or world affairs, there's a more basic risk: If growth investments are poorly chosen, not only may there be no growth, but you can easily lose money instead of making it.

So in opening and managing a brokerage IRA, your choices are more critical than in opening a bank or money market fund IRA. But you can keep these risks within reasonable limits if (1) you are knowledgeable enough about investments to know how to choose your own investments or work successfully with a broker; or (2) you already have a brokerage account and a broker who has proved satisfactory; or (3) you have been recommended to a broker who has handled investments successfully over a reasonably long period for someone you know.

Choosing a Broker

If you decide to deal with a broker who is strange to you, be careful, and don't hesitate to ask all the questions you can. No question is stupid if it is important to you. Handling investments is a difficult art. The broker may be honest and sincere, but his or her other basic function is that of a salesperson for the brokerage firm, and he or she may or may not have the judgment and expertise needed to do a good job for you. Choose carefully.

However, if you feel uncertain about the available brokers, don't feel disadvantaged. Most of the same investment growth possibilities are available through mutual funds. (See Chapter 13.)

In fact, in the early years, when your IRA is small, your broker may recommend investing it in one of the mutual funds offered by the brokerage firm. In the mutual fund, your money will be pooled with that of many others for efficient management and lower cost.

"Self-directed" IRA

As your IRA grows, you can, if you wish, enjoy the choice of what is usually called a "self-directed" IRA. You can then put your money in one or more of the many investments available through your brokerage firm—common stocks, common stock mutual funds, bonds, bond funds, real estate investments, oil and gas investments, etc. Some of these are available through "unit trusts," a pooling arrangement that in some respects resembles a mutual fund, or "limited partnerships," another sort of pooling arrangement.

The self-directed IRA gives you great flexibility, since you can usually switch among the available investments by a simple phone call to your broker. But depending on the type of investment, there may be sizable commission charges or other transaction costs when you make these changes.

Talk to your broker carefully about the fees and commissions involved in a brokerage IRA, and shop carefully.

The firm may charge $25 or more to open an IRA and more than that annually to maintain it. In addition, there will be commission charges to be paid on your individual transactions. The charges should be lower if you are limiting your purchases to mutual funds. Ask about all these charges carefully in advance, especially when your IRA is small, as these charges can eat away a noticeable percentage of your fund. Of course, if you have a broker who gives you outstandingly good advice, the results should be well worth the costs.

If you are an experienced investor and intend to make your own investment choices in a brokerage IRA, you may want to use a "discount broker." A discount broker is a firm that charges cut-rate commissions but does not give the advice or have the research backup that is available through a full-service brokerage firm. Some discount firms are newer and less well tested than the old-line brokerage houses. But since brokerage accounts are insured up to $500,000 by the Securities Investor Protection Corporation (SIPC), there is nothing imprudent about using a discount firm for your IRA. (For more information, see the No Nonsense Financial Guide, *How to Choose a Discount Stockbroker.*)

13 · MUTUAL FUND IRAs

In the preceding chapter we mentioned that brokerage firm IRAs are by no means the only way to invest your IRA for *growth*. Another way, and a way that may be more convenient and practical for most people—and probably less risky—is through mutual funds.

We have already discussed one type of mutual fund, the money market fund. The money funds have become, in a remarkably short time, the best-known type of mutual fund. But another large group of mutual funds invest in common stocks, and still others invest in long-term bonds, tax-exempt securities, and more specialized types of investments. (For a full discussion of mutual funds, read the No Nonsense Financial Guide, *Understanding Mutual Funds.*)

As we said, a mutual fund is a way of pooling the money of many investors so that it can be managed efficiently and economically as a single large unit. The principle has been so successful that mutual funds now handle over $300 billion of investors' money (not including over $250 billion in the money market funds).

Because of the large pool of money, a mutual fund can hire the highest quality *professional management*. It can also *diversify* its investments, which means that it can reduce risk by spreading the total investment over many different securities.

The mutual funds also give you *convenience*. Technically, mutual funds are "open-end" investment companies—open-end because they stand ready to sell additional new shares to investors at any time or to buy back ("redeem") shares sold previously. Almost all funds offer simple IRA plans that make it easy for you to start your IRA and invest. The fees you pay for opening and maintaining the account are very small—usually $10 to $15 a year or less.

You can start a mutual fund IRA with as little as $250 and your investment always receives its full share of interest and dividends. If your fund is part of a larger fund group, you can usually arrange to switch by telephone within the funds in the group—sometimes for no charge at all, sometimes for a small charge, perhaps $5 per transaction. And most funds have toll-free ("800") numbers for added convenience and answers to your questions.

Load vs. No-load

There are "load" mutual funds and "no-load" funds. A "load" fund is generally bought through a broker or salesperson who helps you with your selection and charges a commission ("load")—usually from 4.5 percent to 8.5 percent of the total amount you invest. This means that as little as 91.5 percent of the money you invest is actually applied to buy shares in the pool. In contrast, you choose a no-load fund yourself without the help of a broker or salesperson, but 100 percent of your investment dollars go into the pool for your account.

Which are better—load or no-load funds? That really depends on how much time and effort you want to devote to fund selection and supervision of your investment. Some people have neither the time, inclination nor aptitude to devote to the task—for them, a load fund may be the answer. The load may be well justified by long-term results if your broker or salesperson helps you invest in a fund that performs outstandingly well.

How to Pick a No-Load Fund

If you have decided in favor of no-load funds and intend to make your own selections, just how do you pick the fund or funds that are best for you? The more you intend to concentrate on growth and accept the risks that go with it, the more important it is that you entrust your money only to high-quality, tested managements.

There are several publications that compile figures on mutual fund performance for periods as long as ten or even twenty years. One that is found in many libraries is the *Wiesenberger Investment Companies* annual handbook. The Wiesenberger yearbook is the bible of the fund industry, with extensive descriptions of funds, all sorts of other data, and plentiful performance statistics. You may also have access to the *Lipper Mutual Fund Performance Analysis*, an extensive service subscribed to primarily by professionals. It is issued weekly, with special quarterly issues showing longer-term performance. On the newsstands, *Money* magazine has frequent mutual fund articles and quarterly performance surveys; *Barron's* weekly has quarterly mutual fund issues in mid-February, May, August and November; and *Forbes* magazine runs an excellent annual mutual fund survey issue in August or September. (For additional sources, see the No Nonsense Financial Guide, *Understanding Mutual Funds*.)

These sources (especially Wiesenberger) will also give you descriptions of the funds and their investment policies and objectives. When you have selected several funds that look promising to you, call each fund (most have toll-free "800" numbers) to get the fund's prospectus and recent financial reports. The prospectus is the legal document describing a mutual fund's policies for prospective investors. It may be dry reading, but the prospectus and the reports together should give you a picture of what the fund is trying to do and how well it has succeeded over the last ten years.

Common Stock Funds

Common stock funds are usually classified by the degree of risk they take. These general classifications include "aggressive growth" or "maximum capital gain" funds, those that take the greatest risks in pursuit of maximum growth; "growth" or "long-term growth" funds, which may be a shade lower on the risk scale; and "growth and income" funds, which are generally considered to be middle-of-the-road. There are also common stock "income" funds, which in fact try for some growth as well as income, but stay on the conservative side by investing mainly in established companies that pay sizable dividends to their owners. These also are termed "equity income" funds, and the best of them have achieved excellent growth records.

Whichever of these groups is for you, you will want to pick one or more funds that have performed well relative to other funds in the same risk group. But don't simply pick the fund that happens to have performed best in the previous year; concentrate on the record over five or ten years. A fund that has made its shareholders' money grow favorably over a ten-year period, covering both up and down periods in the stock market, can be considered well tested. It's also worth looking at the year-to-year record within the whole period to see how *consistent* management has been.

You will note that the range of performance over most periods among the different funds is quite wide. Don't be surprised. Managing investments is a difficult art. Fund managers are generally experienced professionals, but their records have ranged from remarkably good to mediocre and, in a few cases, quite poor. Pick carefully.

Your biggest problem in selection will probably be that there are several very fine funds in every risk group, and you obviously can't invest in all of them. Once you have narrowed your choice to a small group of funds with superior records matching your objectives, how to pick one over the others may be a puzzle. If two funds have similar performance records, and if there's nothing in their policies to make you prefer one over the other, then it's virtually impossible to forecast which of the two will do better for you in the future. A perfectly reasonable course is to pick one or two of these funds arbitrarily; stay with them for a year or so; compare them again with the competition; continue with them if they've done well, and switch to others if they haven't. If you are dealing with no-load funds, there's no cost in getting out and no cost in getting in.

Other Types of Mutual Funds

Of course, there are other types of mutual funds in addition to the money funds and common stock funds. There are bond funds that, in effect, lend your money out long-term as opposed to the short-term loans made by the money market funds. (A bond represents long-term debt of a governmental entity or corporation.) Bonds should give you a somewhat higher interest return than the money funds, but you run the risk of price fluctuations as interest rates change. There really is no easy way to judge when bond funds are a good buy and when they aren't (see *Understanding Mutual Funds*). There are also tax-exempt bond funds, both short-term and long-term; but these should never be bought for your IRA, which is already tax exempt.

There are many types of specialized funds. But if you want growth, there is no need to reach for esoteric possibilities. Very few investments of any type have achieved better long-term growth records than the best-performing general common stock funds.

Common stock investments are sometimes in favor and sometimes out of favor, and many people pay too little attention to the possibilities of common stocks. But if your IRA has many years to run, you owe it to yourself to consider the records of the common stock mutual funds and what they have done for their shareholders over the years.

A list of selected larger no-load fund groups follows:

SELECTED MAJOR NO-LOAD MUTUAL FUND GROUPS

Name of Group or Manager	Toll-free Telephone Number
Dreyfus Funds**	800-645-6561
Fidelity Group*	800-544-6666
Financial Programs	800-525-8085

Name of Group or Manager	Toll-free Telephone Number
Neuberger & Berman Management	800-367-0770
T. Rowe Price Funds	800-638-5660
Scudder Funds	800-225-2470
SteinRoe & Farnham Funds	800-621-0320
Twentieth Century Funds*	800-345-2021
USAA Investment Management	800-531-8000
Value Line Group	800-223-0818
Vanguard Group	800-662-7447

*Group also includes one or more low-load funds.
**Group also includes load and low-load funds.

14 · INSURANCE COMPANY IRAs

Insurance companies have always been involved in savings as well as insurance, and it is not surprising that they account for a sizable slice of the IRA dollars invested in recent years. Your insurance agent may already have offered an IRA plan to you. Be careful.

Strip away the trimmings, and most insurance company IRAs have much in common with bank IRAs, from an investment point of view. Your money is invested at a certain rate of interest, which is changed from time to time according to market conditions. While the insurance company will stress the long-term nature of the program, the interest rate you receive at the beginning is not guaranteed for very long—probably not more than one year.

However, all sorts of insurance tie-ins may be added to this basically simple savings program. By law, no part of your deductible IRA contribution may be applied to the purchase of life insurance. But the insurance company plan may include, for example, *plan completion insurance*, under which, if you die before reaching retirement, the insurance company adds to your account whatever additional money you would have contributed up to retirement age. You may also be offered disability insurance, which completes your plan in the same way if you become permanently disabled. There are other special insurance tie-ins that may also be suggested. Finally, when it is time for you to begin taking your money out, the insurance company offers you a choice of payment options that will include a true lifetime annuity option—that is, payments guaranteed to continue for your lifetime or the joint lifetimes of you and your spouse.

These various options may or may not appear useful to you, but it is important to note that you can obtain them, if you wish, without tying them to your IRA. Insurance companies will gladly sell you disability insurance in varying amounts whether or not they have your IRA. If you want extra life insurance protection while your savings (in an insurance company or elsewhere) are beginning to build up, you can buy "term" life insurance, the simplest, cheapest form of life insurance. You can even buy "decreasing term" life insurance, under which the protection starts at a maximum amount and gradually decreases as your savings build up or your need for family protection diminishes.

The lifetime annuity at retirement is an insurance company specialty. But it is available no matter where you keep your IRA. All you need to do, after age 59½, is to withdraw a lump sum from your IRA (any type IRA) and apply it immediately to the purchase of a lifetime annuity from an insurance company. The annuity works no differently than if you had been with the insurance company the whole time. You receive regular payments for your lifetime, or for the combined lifetimes of you and your spouse. You don't pay income tax on the lump sum withdrawn to buy the annuity, but only on the annuity payments as you receive them.

Incidentally, an annuity isn't the only way to be assured of life-long income. Annuities are often rather expensive to the buyer, and their payout may be calculated at relatively low interest rates, as compared to the actual interest rates prevailing in the market. There have been at least some periods in the market when it was clearly more advantageous to buy long-term bonds for lifetime income.

In setting out these warnings, we are suggesting that one disadvantage of the insurance company IRAs is that you may find yourself drawn into paying extra for insurance features that you don't really need. And you may be using money for this purpose that should really be going into your IRA.

There's another objection that may be even more important. We have stressed several times that a major advantage of an IRA retirement and investment plan is that it is *under your control*—and that your IRA can make a major difference to your financial future if you manage it intelligently. But this requires *flexibility*.

Up until now, we have dealt with IRAs that generally give you this flexibility. With a bank, a money fund, a brokerage firm IRA, or a mutual fund, you have flexibility—whenever you change your mind, you can change the way your IRA is invested. (You might, however, have to pay a small penalty to get out of a bank CD that isn't due to mature yet.)

But with an insurance company IRA, you don't have this flexibility. Or at least, you are likely to have to pay a high price for changing. Insurance company savings packages are usually structured so that you pay a penalty if you want to stop, and their IRA plans are no exception. If you decide, three or four years down the road, that you really would like to move half of your IRA money into an aggressive growth fund, the insurance company is likely to charge you a stiff exit fee on the money you take out.

Apart from the dollars you lose, the knowledge that there will be a stiff penalty is likely to be an inhibiting factor. Instead of periodically reanalyzing your investments and freely moving your IRA money to where it will work hardest for you, you may instead find reasons for leaving the money where it is, for better or worse. If you have also bought plan completion or disability insurance, you may hesitate to discontinue them. The freedom that you should have in handling your IRA investment has been severely trimmed.

While we have no particular desire to be critical of insurance companies, there are two more drawbacks to their IRA plans that need to be mentioned. The first has to do with annual fees and charges. Since the insurance company's fee structure has to support your own insurance agent and the rest of the sales force, their fees tend to be considerably higher than those charged by the banks. You may indeed be getting substantial personal help and service, but you are paying for it.

The second problem concerns the rate at which your money earns. Here the practice varies from company to company, but in general, the interest rates paid on insurance IRAs appear to have averaged below those paid by banks for comparable periods. So even if you are sure that you will want to stick with a conservative, interest-earning IRA, and if you are not concerned with being flexible and able to change your investments, the insurance company IRAs still do not warrant a "best buy" rating.

No matter how much you respect your insurance agent, and no matter how good a job he or she has done in the past in planning your *insurance*, think twice and ask careful questions before you let him or her open an IRA for you. Nevertheless, we hasten to state that an insurance company IRA, despite its costs and inflexibility, is far better than no IRA at all. If you really suffer from inertia or indecision so severely that you run the danger of never opening an IRA at all, then by all means open one through your insurance agent.

If you find that you absolutely can't save unless you know that you owe a payment to an insurance company, do likewise and don't worry about the charges. The tax advantages of an IRA are so important to your long-run financial future that an expensive IRA is still far better than no IRA at all.

15 · SPLITTING AND SWITCHING

Flexibility

In discussing insurance company IRAs, we touched on an important subject—the need to be flexible in handling your IRA investments, and the importance of being able to move from one type of investment to another.

Up until now, we have perhaps talked as if each person could find one particular type of IRA that would be just right for him or her. In certain cases, it may work that way. But the probabilities are otherwise.

It's not likely that one particular investment, or one set of investments, will prove suitable indefinitely.

Successful investing requires, above all, that you be flexible—be ready and willing to adjust to changing conditions and opportunities. This holds true as much for your IRA as for any other type of investment. You must *manage* your IRA if you want maximum results. The initial choice of investment is important, but it is only the beginning.

So after you have begun your IRA, you need to take time periodically to *think* about your IRA and how your IRA money is invested. Are you still happy with your first choice? Has there been any change in the economy that would make you want to see your money invested differently? Has there been any change in your own situation? Have you changed your thinking about investments? Do you simply feel that you made a mistake?

Fortunately, the IRA rules are designed to give you all the flexibility you need and to let you manage your IRA investment like a professional.

Multiple IRA Accounts

First, you are not limited to any one investment in your IRA. If you want to spread your IRA over more than one

53

type of investment—and the larger your IRA grows, the more sense this is likely to make—the law puts absolutely no limit on how many different IRA accounts you can have. And in a given year you can contribute to as many different IRAs as you wish, as long as your total combined contributions don't exceed $2,000 (or $2,250 combined for a regular and spousal IRA). The only limits on "splitting" your contributions are the minimums imposed by each plan sponsor.

The law also gives you virtually complete freedom in moving money from one IRA to another. There are certain rules to follow, which we will describe below, but they are quite simple. So you have complete freedom to switch from one investment to another, alter the balance among several different investments, or eliminate an investment entirely if it doesn't suit you.

Why Change?

We need to say a little more about *why* you should make use of all this flexibility. If you have thought hard and considered carefully before you made your first IRA investment, haven't you earned the right to relax and forget it for a while?

That depends. If you are content with safety rather than maximum growth, there may be little need for constant review. Money in a money market fund or bank money market account, if that is what you have chosen, will continue to earn the going rate without any attention on your part. Money in a two- or three-year bank certificate certainly shouldn't require much attention. Yet even here there can be exceptions. Let's say you have invested your IRA money in a longer-term bank certificate, and interest rates have risen sharply. The bank may now be offering much higher rates on certificates. In this case, as suggested in Chapter 10, you should do a careful calculation to see if it would be worth paying the penalty (probably loss of three months' interest) in order to switch out of the old, lower-paying certificate and into a new one at the higher rate.

Review and Rethink

If you are in any kind of growth-oriented investment where the risks are greater, the reasons for review intensify. Let's say you have a brokerage IRA, and have bought a few shares of stock in a new computer company. The company could end up as a blazing success or a bankruptcy case (or occasionally both) in very short order, so you and your broker should both keep a careful eye on it. Common stocks that are considered far less risky—utilities and banks, for example—also have turned into disasters on occasion if left unwatched.

But your investments need to be reviewed and considered even when you think you are taking the least risk possible. What could be safer than U.S. Treasury bonds? No one really doubts that every U.S. government bond will be paid off in full at maturity. But in the 1960s and 1970s, as interest rates in the U.S. rose in a great sweeping upward movement, new bonds were issued at higher and higher rates. The prices of old bonds paying lower rates declined in an equally broad sweep. By 1981, when the disaster was at its worst, perfectly good U.S. Treasury 8 percent bonds were selling at 60 cents on the dollar, 40 percent below their face value. The reason for reciting this story is to point out that these bonds, in many cases, were held through this whole decline by major institutions who suffered untold billions of dollars of losses in their portfolios as a result. Undoubtedly, some of these institutions thought carefully about their bond portfolios and simply made the wrong judgments about economic conditions. But just as undoubtedly, many institutions suffered losses simply because of inertia, carelessness, and an unwise assumption that they could safely continue doing in the future what they had always done in the past.

The moral of this story is—*think!* Your IRA will play a key role in your financial future. A little time spent now in review and management may help make that future considerably brighter and more comfortable.

What to Watch For

When you review your IRA (or any other investments you may have), no one expects you to be a better prophet than the professional economists and market analysts. You probably won't foretell the next decline in bond prices or the next bank collapse. But there are some relatively straightforward things that you can think about and look for.

For example, say that you are age 60, your IRA is invested in two long-term growth mutual funds, and you have just decided that you will retire in two years and begin to take your IRA money out for living expenses. If the growth funds have been doing well and have gone up in value, it may make sense to switch at least part of that money into a bank IRA or money market fund IRA, so that you will have an assured pool of dollars when you are ready to begin withdrawals.

Or take an opposite example. You are age 25, and you began your IRA two years ago at a bank with a simple CD, since that seemed the safest thing to do. Now you have learned more about investments and decided that with more than thirty years ahead in which to build up your IRA, you have the opportunity of accumulating more wealth by investing carefully in common stocks.

Or you may be responding to a change in outside conditions. Perhaps you have invested your money in an aggressive growth mutual fund that has achieved an exceptionally fine long-term growth rate—varying from year to year but averaging close to 20 percent a year over a long period. Now you find that the fund has completed two very good years in a row with a combined gain of 60 percent, and you are worried that the next year will be a poor one and that some of the gain will be lost. So, for protection, you decide to switch half of your value temporarily into a money market fund.

Or perhaps you may simply feel that you have made a mistake. Mistakes happen. Perhaps you picked a money fund and now find that you could have gotten a substantially better return over the last year at your local bank. Perhaps you started an IRA with a brokerage firm and you now feel that you have had poor advice or poor service from the broker.

Certainly you shouldn't make changes in your IRA, or in any other investment, for trivial reasons. But it is important to stay flexible and to be ready and willing to make changes when a serious reason develops. Don't become overly attached to an investment just because it has been successful in the past—it may have been appropriate for one particular time and not for another.

Even more important, don't be afraid to recognize and admit that an investment has done badly, either because you chose poorly or for reasons outside your control. Investing almost always involves uncertainties, and even the best experts make mistakes. The mark of the true professional is being honest enough to recognize a mistake and brave enough to correct it quickly, even if it means taking a loss in the process. It is the mistakes that are not caught quickly that sometimes turn into disasters—like those Treasury bonds we talked about a little earlier.

In addition to being willing to *change* investments, you should consider the merits of *diversifying* your investments, especially as your IRA grows larger. Diversifying is another important way of limiting and controlling your risks. Because of the uncertainties in the market and in the world, it is always possible that any single investment will turn out disappointing. By spreading your investments over several different areas, you reduce the risk that any one disappointment may become a disaster from the standpoint of your total results.

If you invest in a mutual fund, the fund managers, as pointed out in Chapter 13, are already spreading your investment over a large number of securities. You may wish to go a step further. What if you have invested in a growth fund that invests primarily in small, growing companies, and you are afraid that the country is going into a recession that will keep that type of company from making progress for a year or two? The professional response is to make sure that not all your money is exposed to one particular type of risk. So you might move a certain percentage into a different type of common stock fund or into a money market fund until you have a clearer view of the outlook.

How to Diversify

In an IRA, the mechanics involved in doing all these things are relatively simple. Diversifying is easy. As pointed out above, the law lets you have as many different IRAs as you wish, as long as your total contributions to all of them combined don't exceed the legal limit. If you own shares in a money market fund or common stock fund that is part of a larger family of funds, a phone call will probably be sufficient to move part or all of your money to one of the other funds in the group. If you have a brokerage IRA, one of the key advantages is the ability to add or switch investments with a phone call to your broker.

Switching completely out of one IRA investment and into another may or may not be more complicated, depending on how your IRA is set up. In a brokerage IRA, as pointed out above, there's no difficulty—you are not changing from one sponsor to another, but merely changing investments within the plan maintained by the brokerage firm. The same is true if you switch investments from one mutual fund to another within a single family of funds.

On the other hand, if you switch an IRA from a bank to a mutual fund, or from a mutual fund to a brokerage firm, a little more effort is needed. At this point we want to clear up some confusion about this type of switch. You may sometimes hear it referred to as a *rollover*. The term *rollover* has certain very specific meanings with respect to retirement plans and IRAs. In one type of rollover, you are permitted to withdraw money completely from one IRA as long as you put it into another IRA within sixty days. You can only do this type of IRA rollover once a year, and the money *must* be back in another IRA within sixty days, or else you pay income tax on it (plus the penalty tax, if you are under age 59½) exactly as if it had been distributed out completely to you from your IRA.

But there is no need to use this slightly dangerous procedure for switching IRA investments. A much better procedure is not to have the money paid out to you at all, but to have it transferred directly from the trustee or custodian of the first IRA to the trustee or custodian of the second. In this case the switch is usually termed a *transfer* rather than a rollover, and there is no limit on how many times a year you can use this procedure. (In the next chapter, we will discuss a different situation where the rollover procedure is correct and appropriate.)

Most IRA plans have banks as trustees or custodians. To make the kind of switch from one sponsor to another that we have been talking about, write to your old custodian, giving the name and number of your account, and say something like the following:

> Dear Sir or Madam:
>
> I have opened an IRA with the Glocca Morra Income Fund, for which the Rainbow Bank of Western Alabama acts as custodian. Please transfer all the assets of the above IRA account directly to the Rainbow Bank as custodian.
>
> Very truly yours,

Send a copy of the letter to your new plan sponsor (Glocca Morra Income Fund), so that someone there will know the money is coming and can identify it better when it arrives. Your old custodian or trustee will very likely require that your signature, on the above letter of instructions, be "guaranteed" by a commercial bank or brokerage firm. If you have previously been a mutual fund investor, you are probably familiar with this signature guarantee requirement. If you expect to be a consistent investor in the future, it's best to get someone at your commercial bank accustomed to providing you with this service. The guarantee simply confirms the authenticity of the signer—it guarantees that you are who you say you are.

Now the good news about switching your IRA invest-ments: There's never a capital gains tax to pay. Remember, your IRA is tax deferred. No matter what kind of gains you make, the IRS doesn't get its share until you begin to take the money out. So the tax on gains, which sometimes inhibits people from making needed changes in their ordi-nary investments, doesn't need to inhibit you at all in your IRA. Score another point for tax-free compounding!

16 · ROLLOVERS

Now for some words about a more important type of rollover—one that is *not* a switch from one type of IRA to another, but that involves a different and special type of IRA.

This different kind of rollover is important if you get a lump-sum distribution from an "employer's qualified plan," which includes most government, corporate, and self-employed (Keogh) retirement plans. The law says that if you get a lump-sum distribution from such a plan, *you may roll over part or all of the distribution tax free* into an IRA if the rollover is completed within sixty days after the distribution is completed. You pay no income tax on the part of the distribution that is rolled over, until such time as it is withdrawn from the IRA.

A "lump-sum distribution" is defined as distribution of your complete share in your employer's plan within a calendar year. A distribution of this type may occur when you retire or leave your employer, or because you have reached age 59½, or because of disability, or when an employer's plan is discontinued. A distribution that only includes part of your share in your employer's plan can usually also be rolled over into an IRA if the distribution results from separation from service or disability. Any amounts you contributed to your employer's plan are excluded from the rollover, since you have already paid tax on them and are not liable for additional tax on those amounts.

An IRA that is set up with this type of rollover is usually identified by some phrase such as "Special Rollover IRA." There's no dollar limit on these rollovers—it's quite common for a Special Rollover IRA to amount to several hundreds of thousands of dollars. If you have a regular IRA, the two IRAs should be kept separate, and your regular annual contributions should be made to your regular IRA. The Special Rollover IRA carries a special privilege, the ability to roll over the assets again into another employer's qualified plan, which is lost if the account is mixed in with regular IRA contributions.

A word of warning. This type of rollover has gotten considerable publicity, and many people receiving lump-sum distributions from retirement plans have rolled them over into a Special Rollover IRA without considering the possible alternatives. This is usually a good choice, but not always. A lump-sum distribution that is *not* rolled over into an IRA may qualify for a special income tax break ("forward averaging") that could result in the distribution's being taxed at a lower-than-usual rate. But once the distribution is rolled over into an IRA, it is subject to the usual IRA rules and will be taxed at ordinary income tax rates when withdrawn.

If all or most of a lump-sum distribution is rolled over and stays in a Special Rollover IRA for several years, the tax-free compounding will more than make up for this possible tax disadvantage. But if the money only stays in the IRA for a few years before being withdrawn, you may eventually end up with less money after taxes than if you had taken the lump-sum distribution without a rollover and paid tax on it at the special rate. If you receive a lump-sum distribution, it makes sense to talk to a tax adviser before deciding whether or not to roll part or all of it over into a special IRA. (And note that if you roll over *part* of a lump-sum distribution into an IRA, the remainder does *not* qualify for "forward averaging" treatment.)

17 · IRAs WHERE YOU WORK

So far we have talked about IRAs where you take the initiative and set up the account(s) yourself. But some employers have arrangements of various sorts to help you set up an IRA and, in some cases, to pay for it with regular payroll deductions.

If a payroll deduction IRA is available where you work, is it a good idea? Your employer may have made IRA arrangements with a mutual fund group, or with an insurance company. You may have the choice of having your money invested in one or more different types of mutual funds, or in fixed-income or common stock accounts managed by an insurance company. The IRA is still basically and legally yours, and subject to the same rules as any other IRA, and you are paying for it yourself via the payroll deductions. But you may value the convenience, and the employer may possibly be saving you some of the costs and fees that you would otherwise pay.

If this type of arrangement encourages you to have an IRA when you otherwise wouldn't, you are obviously being helped. On the other hand, if you are making a serious choice between a payroll deduction IRA and one you establish on your own, you should try and think not in terms of convenience but in terms of what the IRA will ultimately do for you. The key question, as we have been saying throughout this book, is how your IRA is *invested*. If the payroll deduction IRA includes one or more investment choices comparable to what you would have chosen on your own, then it may work for you. But if you think you can find investments that are better or more comfortable for you, then protect your future by putting your money where you think it will do the most for you over the long run.

The SEP-IRA: A Very Different IRA

An arrangement of a very different sort is the "Simplified Employee Pension," or SEP-IRA. Legally this is classified as a form of IRA, but rather than being a plan you initiate yourself, it is a plan that is initiated by your employer as an alternative to a regular company pension plan. Because it is, in effect, a form of company pension plan, we won't describe all the workings in detail, but there are a few points worth noting.

If you work for a firm where the employer has set up a SEP-IRA, you must generally be covered if you are age 21 or older and have worked for your employer during at least three of the past five years. The employer makes payments into a special SEP-IRA account that you set up *with the sponsor of your choice*—so you do have the same control over investment choices as in a regular IRA. But many of the sponsors who offer regular IRAs have *not* taken the trouble to offer SEP-IRAs, which require a separate procedure on the sponsor's part. So you may have to shop around in order to set up a SEP-IRA account (or accounts) that give you the investment approach you want.

The employer's contributions are not subject to the $2,000 annual limitation, but fall under the much higher limits governing contributions to employer pension plans. You can still have your own IRA, quite separate from the SEP-IRA, and contribute up to $2,000 to it, subject to all the usual rules; or, for convenience, you are permitted to put your $2,000 (or less) in the SEP-IRA account.

In either case, since you are covered by your employer under the SEP-IRA, your own contribution will be tax-deductible only if you are below the income limits explained in Chapter 3.

Salary Reduction Plans

Because of the restrictions on the IRA tax deduction, an increasing number of firms are offering *salary reduction* plans, under which you agree to have your employer withhold a certain part of your pay and deposit it into a retirement plan, and you are *not* taxed on that part of your compensation. You can see that this arrangement has much the same effect as making a tax-deductible IRA contribution, except that the salary reduction plans often permit much bigger contributions than in an IRA.

The much-talked-about "401(k)" plans are employer profit-sharing plans with a salary reduction feature. Smaller firms now also have the alternative of building a salary reduction arrangement into a SEP-IRA. Employees of schools and nonprofit organizations are often offered "403(b)" plans which involve the same salary reduction feature.

If one of these plans is offered where you work, consider the advantages of setting aside part of your pay tax free. And if you can't afford both a salary reduction arrangement and an IRA contribution, compare the two carefully. If your IRA contribution will not be tax-deductible, the salary reduction plan has an obvious advantage. Even if you are at an income level where an IRA contribution *is* tax-deductible, the salary reduction arrangement may be preferable. First, in a 401(k) plan, your permitted contribution is likely to be larger than with an IRA—potentially as high as $7,000, depending on your salary level and the terms of the plan. Second, your employer may choose to make matching contributions on some percentage basis. Third, depending on its terms, the plan may permit you to borrow from it, which is not permitted in an IRA. Finally, at retirement, if you wish, you may be able to take advantage of the special tax treatment for lump-sum distributions from qualified plans, which is not available to IRAs. So if you can't afford to contribute to both, the odds seem to be stacked in favor of the salary reduction plan, particularly if your employer is making a matching contribution of any appreciable size. But there are still a few points to watch. How will your money be invested in a 401(k) plan? An inadequate choice of investments can cancel out all the advantages. Also, you don't have the control and flexibility you have in an IRA. In an IRA, you can always decide to take your money out, paying the 10 percent penalty tax if necessary; and the choice of investments, as we have emphasized and reemphasized in this book, is completely yours.

Other types of savings plans may be offered by your employer. Since the possible variations are wide, the only good advice is to review the terms of any such plan carefully and compare it with what you can accomplish through your own IRA.

We have not specifically mentioned self-employed retirement plans, popularly known as "Keogh" plans, which now carry most of the same features as corporate retirement plans. If you work for a single proprietor or a partnership with a Keogh plan in effect, your situation is the same as if you were covered under a corporate retirement plan; your IRA contributions will be tax-deductible only if your income is below the specified levels.

If you yourself are a self-employed businessman or professional, you can have an IRA as well as a Keogh plan. But if you are in a high income bracket, the IRA may make little sense, since you can make large contributions to a Keogh plan which will be fully tax-deductible. (For more information on Keogh plans, see the No Nonsense Financial Guide, *How to Plan and Invest for Your Retirement.*)

18 · THINGS YOU CAN'T DO

In this book we have talked mainly about all the profitable things that an IRA allows you to do. Now a brief chapter on the things you *can't* do.

Some of these have been mentioned earlier. There are certain specific IRA penalty taxes that the IRS imposes. First, as stated earlier, if you withdraw part or all of your IRA money before age 59½, you pay a flat penalty tax of 10 percent of the amount withdrawn, in addition to paying ordinary income tax on the withdrawal. (As explained in Chapter 8, the penalty doesn't apply in case of death, disability, or certain types of periodic payments.) Second, if you overcontribute to your IRA in any given year, and don't withdraw the excess amount before your tax return is due, you pay a 6 percent "excise tax" on the excess amount for each year that it is in the account until it is either withdrawn or applied to make up part of a legitimate contribution in a subsequent year.

Third, there is a tax if you don't begin taking out money at a fast enough rate when you reach age 70½. As we explained in Chapter 7, that is when you must begin taking withdrawals either in a lump sum, by purchase of a lifetime annuity, or by scheduling regular payments over a period not allowed to be longer than your statistical life expectancy or the joint life expectancies of you and your beneficiary. If the amount you withdraw in any year is less than the amount called for by these rules, the amount by which your distribution falls short is called an "excess accumulation," and you pay a *50 percent* excise tax on it. However, you may be excused from the tax if you can convince the IRS that you were wrongly advised or that you made a legitimate mistake.

If you owe any of these penalty taxes, you must file IRS Form 5329 together with the tax owed, even if you aren't required to file a regular income tax return for that year.

Oh yes. You must also file Form 5329 and pay a 15 percent "excise tax" on any distributions from an IRA, or from any combination of retirement plans, which exceed certain very high ceiling levels. Since this tax doesn't apply unless your distributions exceed $150,000 a year (or much higher on a lump-sum distribution), it isn't likely to be a problem for most of us—in fact, many of us would like nothing better than to be in a position where we had to deal with this particular problem.

There are other types of infractions where the law comes down on you more harshly. If you engage in certain "prohibited transactions," your whole IRA loses its tax-exempt status and is treated as having been distributed to you as of the first of the year. You not only owe income tax on the whole IRA, but also the 10 percent penalty tax if you are under age 59½. The actions that can trigger this disaster are (1) borrowing from your IRA, (2) selling property to your IRA, and (3) receiving unreasonable compensation for managing your IRA.

If you don't borrow directly from your IRA, but use part of your IRA as *collateral* for a loan, the part you use as collateral is treated as having been distributed to you, and you must pay tax on it.

You are not allowed to invest any of your IRA money in "collectibles," which are defined as art works, metals, gems, coins, stamps, antiques and (the IRS has thought of everything) alcoholic beverages. Any amount you invest in any of these items is treated as having been distributed to you, with the usual taxes payable. However, you *can* invest in new gold and silver coins issued by the U.S. Government.

As you can see, this wasn't a long chapter. The IRA prohibitions are small (and not unreasonable), the flexibility is wide, and the possibilities are great.

19 · FEES AND FULL DISCLOSURE

We have touched rather lightly in this book on the fees that must be paid to sponsors for opening and maintaining your IRA. Bank fees for IRAs are almost always small and sometimes nonexistent. Money market fund and other mutual fund fees also are usually small enough so that you don't have to worry about them.

With brokerage firm and insurance company IRAs, we have warned you that the fees may be sizable and that you should study them carefully. Obviously, you should avoid dealing with any organization that is not clear and straightforward about the fees they intend to charge. If they are at all hesitant about spelling out their charges, you should be hesitant about paying them.

To what extent should you let the fees influence your choice of IRAs? We have repeatedly recommended that you stress *long-term investment results* in making decisions about your IRA. Are the fees important? The answer depends on the size of your IRA. Let's say that you have set yourself a long-term goal of making your IRA money grow at a rate between 10 percent and 15 percent annually. In the first year you begin with a $2,000 contribution. If you pay starting and maintenance fees that total $50, you have sliced off 2½ percent of your money before you begin, which is a sizable piece of your hoped-for growth. On the other hand, if you contribute and invest successfully for five years and your IRA has grown to $15,000, the same $50 charge would represent well under 1 percent (actually 0.33 percent), and even charges totaling $150 would only represent 1 percent of your fund. A 1 percent charge probably shouldn't bother you if you believe you are in an IRA arrangement that is giving you superior results. But above the 1 percent, you should think carefully about whether the benefits you are getting are substantial enough to be worth the charges.

A small tip. In many cases these processing and maintenance fees are deducted automatically from your IRA account on some preestablished schedule. But in other cases you may be able to pay these charges with a separate personal check, outside the IRA account. This has two advantages. The payment doesn't reduce your IRA account and, if you itemize your income tax deductions and have large "miscellaneous deductions," you may be able to deduct the payment as an investment expense. If the fees are worth being concerned about, check this possibility of separate payment with your IRA sponsor.

The subject of getting adequate information from your plan sponsor requires a special note. Most IRA sponsors do a reasonably good job of providing you with full descriptions of their plans, telling you in detail what you are getting into, including the fees and charges. The law requires an IRA sponsor to give you a full "disclosure statement" describing its plan in detail, including fees and charges and provisions for cancellation. The law also requires that you be given seven days to consider any IRA plan before your investment becomes final. Either the sponsor must give you the disclosure statement seven days before you make your purchase, or the plan must provide you with seven days *after* your purchase in which you can cancel at will and have all your money returned. Beware of signing a plan application in which you acknowledge having received the disclosure statement seven days previously unless you really *did* receive it as stated, or unless you are willing to give up this seven-day right of cancellation.

20 · HAPPY RETIREMENT!

If we were to pick a second title for this chapter, it would be "Keep Your Eye on the Ball."

If you have read this book carefully, you now know all that you probably need to know about the rules governing your IRA. And if you want to learn more about some of the rules that apply in special cases, you can get IRS Publication 590, *Individual Retirement Arrangements*, available free from your local IRS office (it is more readable than you might expect).

But knowing the rules is only a beginning. As we have stressed to the point where you are no doubt tired of hearing it, your IRA is an *investment*. No single book can make you an expert on investments, but we have tried to make clear the different approaches you can take, and have given you guidance on finding the specific IRA investments that will be right for you.

Remember that you have only *begun*. Remember that any investment must be *managed*. You should *think* about your IRA regularly—not only at tax time. As time goes by, conditions will vary, you will learn more about investing, and your attitudes may change. Consider carefully what levels of uncertainty and risk you are willing to live with. Within those limits, think whether you are doing everything you can to improve the growth of your IRA.

If your tendency is to be conservative, consider the risks you may run by *not* being a bit more adventurous. If your IRA has many years to run, you will want it to grow enough to offset the shrinkage in value caused by inflation. Consider that Social Security benefits may not be as generous in the future as they have been in the past. Consider whatever other pension coverage you have, what personal savings, what other assets. Since your IRA grows tax free, you can use it flexibly to fill out your own financial picture in whatever direction seems most important.

If you feel cautious, and hesitate to take the risks involved in trying for higher growth, remember that it doesn't have to be all one or the other. You can start with most of your money in a bank or money market fund, and put a small amount in a growth or growth-income type mutual fund. In the future, you may find yourself becoming more familiar and comfortable with investments that vary in price and with growth rates that may fluctuate sharply from year to year. Eventually, as your IRA grows larger, you may even feel that you want a brokerage IRA to give you the widest possible choice of investments.

Or it may work the other way, and you may find that you are only happy with the security and certainty you can get from bank certificates of deposit. That is why we have talked about finding not just the right investments, but the investments that are right for *you*. Even with the most conservative investments, an IRA provides a boon to your financial future that it would be foolish to miss.

The following numbers will help you see what your choices can mean. The tables show how your money can build up in an IRA at different growth rates. The tables assume that every year you put in either $500, $1,000, or $2,000, with the investment always made at the beginning of the year—which is the best way to do it, if you can.

The tables are clear enough. But one thing they don't show is how little the IRA has cost you. For example, an investment of $1,000 per year over thirty years, growing at only 5 percent, will build up to a value of close to $70,000. But your cost—the money you actually put in—was only $30,000 (30 × $1,000). And if you were able to take tax deductions on your contributions, your real cost was well below $30,000.

At higher growth rates, the difference between cost and results is even more dramatic. Consider the IRA investor who puts in $2,000 per year and invests successfully enough to achieve a 12 percent growth rate over 30 years. His or her nest egg of $540,585 only cost $60,000. If he or she was in a 28 percent tax bracket while making the contributions, and was able to take the full tax deduction, the deductions would have totaled $16,800 (28 percent × $60,000), and the net cost of the IRA would have been only $43,200.

For most of us, an IRA is an opportunity that is hard to equal.

Even the most conservative investor will benefit from the rewards produced by tax-free compounding. And, if you are fortunate enough to achieve higher earnings, your results can be truly remarkable. Use the opportunity!

TAX-FREE COMPOUNDING IN YOUR IRA
Table A: $2,000 per Year

Value at End of Year After:	Growth Rate					
	5%	6%	8%	10%	12%	14%
1 Year	$2,100	$2,120	$2,160	$2,200	$2,240	$2,280
5 Years	11,604	11,951	12,672	13,431	14,230	15,070
10 Years	26,414	27,943	31,291	35,062	39,309	44,089
20 Years	69,439	77,985	98,846	126,005	161,397	207,537
30 Years	139,522	167,603	244,692	361,887	540,585	813,474
40 Years	253,680	328,095	559,562	973,704	1,718,285	3,059,817

TAX-FREE COMPOUNDING IN YOUR IRA
Table B: $1,000 per Year

Value at End of Year After:	Growth Rate					
	5%	6%	8%	10%	12%	14%
1 Year	$1,050	$1,060	$1,080	$1,100	$1,120	$1,140
5 Years	5,802	5,975	6,336	6,716	7,115	7,535
10 Years	13,207	13,972	15,646	17,531	19,655	22,045
20 Years	34,720	38,993	49,423	63,003	80,698	103,768
30 Years	69,761	83,802	122,346	180,944	270,293	406,737
40 Years	126,840	164,048	279,781	486,852	859,143	1,529,909

TAX-FREE COMPOUNDING IN YOUR IRA
Table C: $500 per Year

Value at End of Year After:	Growth Rate					
	5%	6%	8%	10%	12%	14%
1 Year	$525	$530	$540	$550	$560	$570
5 Years	2,901	2,988	3,168	3,358	3,558	3,768
10 Years	6,604	6,986	7,823	8,766	9,827	11,022
20 Years	17,360	19,496	24,712	31,501	40,349	51,884
30 Years	34,881	41,901	61,173	90,472	135,146	203,369
40 Years	63,420	82,024	139,891	243,426	429,571	764,954

APPENDIX A
YOUR INCOME LEVEL AND
YOUR IRA DEDUCTION

Before 1987, all IRA contributions were tax-deductible. But the Tax Reform Act of 1986, which took effect in 1987, changed the rules, as explained in Chapter 3. Here are the current rules regarding IRA deductions, in somewhat more detail than was provided in Chapter 3:

If you are single, and you are *not* covered under any employer's retirement plan, your IRA contributions continue to be *fully tax-deductible*, just as they were before 1987.

If you are married, and neither you nor your spouse is covered under an employer's retirement plan, all IRA contributions by you and/or your spouse also continue to be *fully tax-deductible*. But if you *are* covered under an employer's retirement plan—or if your spouse is covered, and you file a joint income tax return*—then the size of your income determines whether you can take a full deduction for your IRA contribution, a partial deduction, or no deduction.

The size of your income is measured by your "modified AGI." If you file Form 1040A, this is the amount on the Page 1 "Total Income" line. If you file your tax return on Form 1040, your modified AGI is your adjusted gross income before taking any deduction for IRA contributions (and before any foreign earned income exclusion or foreign housing exclusion or deduction).

For individuals or couples with coverage under an employer's retirement plan, here's how the tax deduction

---

*Legislation has been introduced in Congress which would make the income limitations effective for married couples even if they file separate returns.

works, depending on your tax filing status and your modified AGI:

If Your Tax *filing status is:*	You Are Entitled to:		
	A full deduction if AGI is no more than:	A partial deduction if AGI is within the "phase-out" range of:	No deduction if AGI is:
(A)	(B)	(C)	(D)
Single, or Head of Household	$25,000	$25,000–$35,000	$35,000 or more
Married filing a joint return, or Qualifying widow(er)	$40,000	$40,000–$50,000	$50,000 or more
Married filing a separate return	0	0–$10,000	$10,000 or more

The amount in Column B of the above table is called the "threshold" level. If your income is below the threshold, you can deduct a full IRA contribution of $2,000, assuming that your earned income is at least $2,000. But for every $50 of income above the threshold, your deduction is reduced by $10. (However, if your AGI is in the range of $9,000–$9,999 above the threshold, you are allowed a flat deduction of $200.)

Here's a worksheet for figuring your partial deduction:

1. From Column "D" of the above table, enter the appropriate figure, depending on your tax filing status ($35,000, $50,000, or $10,000). _____
2. Enter your modified AGI. _____

3. Subtract #2 from #1. If the result is $10,000 or more, you are entitled to a full IRA deduction. If #2 is greater than #1, you are not entitled to any deduction. If the answer is between $1 and $9,999, go on to step #4.

4. Multiply line #3 by 20% (.20) to get your maximum partial deduction. If the result is not a multiple of $10, round it up to the next highest multiple of $10. (For example, $380.50 is rounded to $390.) However, if the result is less than $200 but more than 0, enter $200.

Of course, if your earned income is below $2,000, your IRA contribution is limited to the amount of your earned income. In that case, your tax deduction also obviously cannot be greater than your earned income, no matter what the above calculation shows.

Deductible and Nondeductible Contributions

Let's say that your earned income is above $2,000 and that the above calculation shows that you are entitled to a tax deduction of $800 on your IRA contribution. If you wish, you can limit your IRA contribution to $800, and take a tax deduction for that amount. But you can also contribute up to the $2,000 limit, in which case the amount above $800 (up to $1,200) becomes a *nondeductible contribution.*

If you make a nondeductible contribution, you must file IRS Form 8606 with your tax return. The form is simple and should not cause you any difficulty. Its purpose is to let the IRS track your nondeductible contributions, since, if you make nondeductible contributions, you will eventually be able to withdraw these amounts from your IRA tax-free. (See Appendix C.)

When Both Spouses Work

If both spouses work, and each has a separate IRA, the above calculation applies to each spouse separately. If the amount on line #4 of the worksheet is $1,500, each spouse could make a deductible contribution of up to $1,500 for the year (assuming that each spouse has earned income of at least $1,500), and the combined deduction of $3,000 would be shown on the couple's joint return. (Each spouse could also make a *nondeductible* contribution of up to $500.) If one spouse contributes less than the permitted deduction, the excess cannot be used by the other spouse; the deduction limit for the other spouse remains the same.

Spousal IRAs

If a spousal IRA is set up for a nonworking or low-income spouse, and the modified AGI of the couple falls in the phase-out range ($40,001–$49,999), a separate calculation must be made to figure the allowable tax deduction. Instructions for this calculation are given in the instructions for Form 1040 and Form 1040A, and also in IRS publication 590, *Individual Retirement Arrangements*.

Optional Nondeductible Contributions

A taxpayer may choose to treat an IRA contribution, or part of a contribution, as nondeductible, even if it is deductible under the rules. See Appendix C.

APPENDIX B
ARE YOU COVERED BY
AN EMPLOYER'S
RETIREMENT PLAN?

Appendix A explained how your IRA tax deduction may be curtailed if you are covered under an employer's retirement plan. How do you determine whether you are "covered" or not?*

You are generally "covered" if you participate in almost any type of company or government retirement plan, such as a qualified pension or profit-sharing plan, Keogh plan, simplified employee pension (SEP), section 401(k) plan, section 403(b) plan, etc. However, you are *not* considered covered merely because of any of the following conditions:

1. You are covered under Social Security.
2. You are covered under Railroad Retirement.
3. You are receiving retirement benefits from a previous employer's plan.
4. You participate in a state or local government deferred compensation plan (a "section 457" plan).
5. You participate in a plan as an Armed Forces reservist but you have less than 90 days of active duty during the year.
6. You participate in a government plan as a volunteer firefighter.

Usually it is not difficult to know whether you are "covered" or not. In case of doubt, your employer should be able to tell you. (Incidentally, in the Form W-2 "Wage and Tax Statement" you receive at the end of the year, the

---

*Another way of phrasing the question is whether or not you are an "active participant" in an employer's retirement plan.

box labeled "Pension Plan" should have been checked by your employer if you were covered for the year.)

However, there are some borderline cases which can be confusing. The rules differ depending on whether your employer's plan is a "defined benefit" plan or a "defined contribution" plan. A *defined benefit plan* is one in which you are entitled to a specified or "determinable" benefit at retirement (for example, a certain dollar amount per month, or a certain percentage of your pre-retirement pay, etc.). In a *defined contribution plan*, your retirement benefit is not specified, but contributions are made to the plan under some rule or formula, and your ultimate benefits depend on the size of these contributions and how the money is invested and grows until retirement. Examples of defined contribution plans are profit-sharing plans, 401(k) plans (actually a specific type of profit-sharing plan), SEPs, etc.

Defined Benefit Plans

If your employer has a defined benefit plan, you are considered "covered" if you are basically eligible to participate in the plan, even if you choose not to be covered, or you do not make a contribution required for participation, or you fail to meet a specified minimum service requirement.

Note that the "plan year" of a plan may not be the calendar year. The rule is that you are "covered" for a given tax year if you are eligible to participate in the plan for the plan year that ends *with or within* your tax year.

Defined Contribution Plans

If your employer's plan is a defined contribution plan, you are "covered" for a tax year only if a contribution by your employer, or a contribution by you, or a forfeiture* actu-

---

*A "forfeiture" occurs in certain cases when an individual leaves a plan and all or part of his/her account is reallocated among the remaining participants.

ally is allocated to your account (for the plan year that ends with or within your tax year). In this case, merely being eligible for the plan does not make you "covered," unless there is an actual allocation to your account.

Vesting

If, under the specifications described above, you are covered by either a defined benefit plan or a defined contribution plan, then you are considered covered whether or not your benefits are "vested"—that is, whether or not you have been in the plan long enough to have acquired a claim on benefits that cannot be forfeited even if you leave your job.

APPENDIX C
CALCULATING YOUR TAXABLE AND NONTAXABLE IRA DISTRIBUTIONS

We have stated the rule that IRA distributions are generally taxable as ordinary income. But if you have made *nondeductible contributions* to an IRA, part of your IRA *distributions* will be *nontaxable*.

In this case, you will eventually receive total nontaxable distributions that exactly equal the dollar total of your nondeductible contributions. But you can't choose which distributions will be nontaxable. Instead, the IRS gives you a formula by which a certain portion of each distribution is nontaxable. Eventually, under the formula, you will receive back all your nondeductible contributions as nontaxable distributions. (However, the *earnings* on your nondeductible contributions will be fully taxable on withdrawal.)

The calculation is made on Form 8606, entitled *Nondeductible IRA Contributions, IRA Basis, and Nontaxable IRA Distributions*—the same form that you must use to report any nondeductible contributions. You should follow Form 8606 for details, but the basic calculation, in slightly simplified form, is as follows:

a) Enter your "IRA Basis"—the total nondeductible IRA contributions you made in all years up to the end of this tax year, reduced by any tax-free withdrawals taken in prior years.   _____

b) Enter the total dollar value of all your IRAs as of the end of the tax year.   _____

c) Enter the total amount of IRA distributions you received during the tax year, excluding any amount subsequently rolled back into an IRA.   _____

d) Enter total of (b) and (c). _____
e) Divide (a) by (d) and enter result as a decimal (to two places). _____
f) Multiply (c) by (e) and enter result. This is the amount of your nontaxable distributions for the tax year. _____
g) Subtract (f) from (c). The difference is your *taxable* distributions to be shown on page 1 of Form 1040. _____

The Nondeductible Option

Even if part or all of your IRA contribution is deductible, you can *choose* to earmark it as nondeductible. You might choose to do this in a year when your income is low; or when other large deductions have put you in a low tax bracket; or in order to lessen your possible exposure to the 10% penalty tax on withdrawals before age 59½ (see below). You forgo the tax deduction now in order to be able to withdraw the money on a nontaxable basis later on.

The Penalty Tax

If you receive an IRA distribution which is subject to the 10% penalty tax because you are under age 59½, any portion of the distribution which is nontaxable under the rules discussed above is also not subject to the penalty tax. So if *all* your contributions are nondeductible, the penalty tax can only apply to that part of your withdrawals representing earnings built up within the IRA.

GLOSSARY

Adviser See Investment Adviser.

Automatic Reinvestment A plan by which income dividends and/or capital gains distributions are automatically applied to buy additional shares of a mutual fund or other security.

Bond A long-term debt security issued by a government or corporation promising repayment of a given amount by a given date, plus interest.

Bond Fund A mutual fund investing primarily in bonds.

Book Shares Shares of a fund owned by an investor and recorded on the books of a fund without a certificate being issued.

Broker-Dealer See Brokerage Firm.

Brokerage Firm A term including several types of firms in the securities business who usually do business with the public.

Capital Wealth invested or available for investment.

Capital Gain The profit from sale of a security or other asset at a price above its cost.

Capital Gains Distribution A payment by a mutual fund to its shareholders derived from capital gains realized by the fund on sales of securities in its portfolio.

Common Stock A security representing a share of ownership in a corporation.

Common Stock Fund A mutual fund investing primarily in common stocks.

Custodian   The organization (usually a bank) responsible for holding your IRA plan assets in safekeeping. Also the organization that holds in safekeeping the securities and other assets of a mutual fund.

Diversification   The practice of spreading investments over several different securities to reduce risk.

Dividend   A share of earnings paid to a shareholder by a mutual fund or other corporation.

Dividend Reinvestment   See Automatic Reinvestment.

Individual Retirement Account   *IRA*—See this whole book.

Investment Adviser   The organization that a mutual fund or other investor pays for investment advice. In the case of a mutual fund, the adviser is usually also the sponsor, promoter, and general business manager of the fund.

Investment Advisory Fee   The fee paid by a mutual fund (or other investor) to an adviser.

Investment Company   A company in which many investors pool their money for investment. Mutual funds are the most popular type.

Liquid Asset Fund   A money market fund.

Liquid Investment   An investment that can be converted easily into cash, without penalty.

Load   The sales charge or commission charged on purchase of some mutual funds.

Money Market Fund   A mutual fund that aims at maximum safety, liquidity, and (usually) a constant price for its shares. Its assets are invested to earn current market interest rates on the safest, short-term, highly liquid investments.

Municipal Bond   A bond issued by a state or local government. The interest is usually exempt from federal income tax.

Mutual Fund   An open-end investment company that pools the investments of many investors to provide them with professional management, diversification, and other advantages.

Net Asset Value   In a mutual fund, the market value of the securities and other assets underlying each share of the fund.

No-Load Fund   A mutual fund that sells its shares at net asset value, without any commission.

Open-End Investment Company   A mutual fund. Technically called "open-end" because the fund stands ready to sell new shares to investors or to buy back shares submitted for redemption.

Portfolio   The total list of securities owned by a mutual fund or by any investor.

Portfolio Manager   An individual who makes decisions regarding buying, selling, or holding securities for an investment organization.

Principal   The capital or main body of an investment, as distinguished from the income earned on it.

Prospectus   The official document describing a mutual fund and offering its shares for sale.

Redemption   The procedure by which a mutual fund buys back shares from shareholders on demand.

Rollover   See Chapters 15 and 16.

SEC   The U.S. Securities and Exchange Commission: The federal agency charged with regulating securities markets and the investment industry.

Security General term meaning stocks, bonds and other investment instruments.

SEP-IRA See Chapter 17.

Stock A security representing an ownership interest in a corporation.

Yield The return on an investment. In securities, the dividends or interest received, usually expressed as an annual percentage of either the current market value or the cost of the investment.

INDEX

ABOUT THE AUTHORS

ARNOLD CORRIGAN, noted financial expert, is the author of *How Your IRA Can Make You a Millionaire* and is a frequent guest on financial talk shows. A senior officer of a large New York investment advisory firm, he holds Bachelor's and Master's degrees in economics from Harvard and has written for *Barron's* and other financial publications.

PHYLLIS C. KAUFMAN, the originator of the *No Nonsense Guides*, is a Philadelphia attorney and theatrical producer. A graduate of Brandeis University, she was an editor of the law review at Temple University School of Law. She is listed in *Who's Who in American Law, Who's Who of American Women, Who's Who in Finance and Industry,* and *Foremost Women of the Twentieth Century.*